THE HABIT OF GRATEFUL

A Handbook for Gratitude

THE HABIT OF GRATEFUL

A HANDBOOK FOR GRATITUDE

KRISTINE NEWELL

NEW DEGREE PRESS

COPYRIGHT © 2022 KRISTINE NEWELL

THE HABIT OF GRATEFUL

A Handbook for Gratitude

ISBN   *979-8-88926-614-3* *Paperback*

            979-8-88926-616-7 *Hardcover*

            979-8-88926-615-0   *Ebook*

To the givers,
thank you.

To my children,
you inspire me.

To my love,
you are my everything.

To my family and friends,
you are my guiding light.

To all the mothers,
keep going.

Foreword

By Bob Burg

The following statement might seem rather bold, or perhaps even a bit "out there"...at least before you read the magnificent book you have in your hands.

"Gratitude" is *the* one habit that makes happiness possible.

What? How can I say that?

Here's how I see it:

You may have an almost uncountable number of blessings in your life, including (but certainly not limited to) the ability to see, hear, touch, taste, and smell. You may have a roof over your head, a meal to eat, a job with which you can pay your bills, a family you love and who loves you, a beautiful sunset to watch, a steaming cup of hot coffee or tea as delicious as it is comforting, and much, much more.

Yes, you might have all this, but if you don't appreciate it—if you're not grateful for it—it's pretty much the same as not having it, and you simply cannot be happy, joyful, and content.

On the other hand, when you live "in gratitude" (rather than "ingratitude") you are indeed happier. This not only feels a lot better, but it also makes you more attractive to others. Yes, happiness is attractive. People are much more likely to want to be around you, to be in relationship with you, to work with you, to do business with you, and to tell others about you.

To "appreciate" is to increase in value. Whatever you appreciate does exactly that: it increases.

Appreciate all your blessings and they increase in value.

The same holds true when it comes to the others in your life, whether family or friends, associates, colleagues, customers, or the person at the customer service counter.

When you "appreciate" a person and, just as importantly, communicate that appreciation to them (however and in whatever way you choose), you actually help them to rise in value, both in your mind and, even more importantly, in their *own* mind.

WOW! Talk about creating value!

And when you appreciate them, *you* appreciate (i.e., gain in value in their mind).

Everything written thus far is truly just the beginning of all the benefits gratitude and appreciation can bring you. You'll learn much more as you read *The Habit of Grateful*.

Rather than tell you about what's in this exquisite book, however, I want to tell you just a bit about the person who wrote it.

Kristine Newell fills me with gratitude just by the very fact that I have the honor and privilege of calling her my friend.

She is an extraordinary human being because she decided to do what it took to become extraordinary.

It's not just the work she put in regarding learning her craft (which she certainly did) and becoming a highly respected top producer, leader, and authority in her field.

It's the work she put in mentally and emotionally.

At the very lowest and darkest point of her life, when all seemed lost, she learned about the importance of gratitude and appreciation. And while I cannot even imagine what it took for her to "will herself" to begin living in gratitude at a time she might have felt anything but, that is exactly what she did.

As a result, she grew. And she continued to grow. And she kept on growing, all the time forming a habit of living in gratitude regardless of the circumstances.

Yes, she has succeeded wildly in all the important ways success can be measured: financially, physically, spiritually, mentally, emotionally, socially, and relationally.

She genuinely, authentically, and transparently shares the downs as well as the ups in this gripping and at times heart-wrenching account of her life's journey.

Personally, I am so proud of her. And I'm in awe of her!

The Habit of Grateful is a game changer...and a life changer.

Buckle your seat belt because you're going to learn some things that, while perhaps a bit counterintuitive, will help you to become the person you know you were meant to be.

Most of all, what you'll learn from Kristine is that an "attitude of gratitude"—far from being some worn out motivational platitude—is actually the key to a financially successful and personally fulfilling life overflowing with happiness and joy!

Wishing you "The Habit of Grateful"!

Bob Burg

Coauthor, *The Go-Giver* and *Go-Giver* Book Series

Author's Note

A young woman asked me if I would recommend a book on how to practice gratitude. I came up with a list of about ten books. The more I thought about it, I wished I had something simple to give her. A handbook of sorts.

So, after being asked the same question over and over, I decided to write a book.

This book is a hybrid of how to practice gratitude as a habit *and* my personal story. Positive thinking changed me forever and helped me climb out of a deep dark hole. I am not a scientist or mental health professional. I have simply gathered this book bit by bit, like walking through fields and harvesting the best ideas. Thank you to everyone that gave me their time, stories, and knowledge.

The *Habit of Grateful* changed the trajectory of my life. I hope you will reap the benefits of a life filled with gratitude. To protect the privacy of others, I have changed a few names and altered some details.

Thank you for reading my work.
With deep gratitude,
Kristine

The Habit of Grateful: A Handbook for Gratitude

Introduction

"Gratitude unlocks the fullness of life. It turns what we have into enough and more. It turns denial into acceptance, chaos to order, confusion to clarity. It can turn a meal into a feast, a house into a home, a stranger into a friend."

—MELODY BEATTIE

Dinner. Focus.

Fall crept into the corners of our old, drafty farmhouse. Sweatshirts and backpacks hung from chairs like casualties around the kitchen table and stacks of dirty dishes spread from the sink onto the counter. The dogs barked and nipped at each other and my three kids (two with soccer cleats on) ran in and out of the kitchen, tracking dirt everywhere.

This was week four of the "mom only show." My husband had just moved out. I was officially a single mom and on my own.

"When is dinner?" my oldest asked.

"I'm hungry," Amelia said, banging open the cabinets and looking for a snack.

"I am working on it."

I was tired. My mind raced thinking of the chores ahead. Dinner, helping kids with homework, and filling out school forms. Cleaning the house—it was always a mess. Then my actual work as a busy real estate agent. And my coursework. I was trying to finish my degree and had two classes that seemed constantly neglected.

This thing called "divorce." It was guilt on my shoulders; a new jacket I wasn't used to. It was too tight around my arms, but too late to return it. My daily mood was tied to my bank account balance which hovered right around $100. Sometimes underwater, sometimes bobbing right at the zero line. I tried not to think of overdraft fees or the certified letters on top of my desk.

I looked in the freezer. There had to be something I could whip up for dinner. It was empty except for frozen veggies and a few old raviolis with freezer burn. Maybe the raviolis didn't look that bad. Did I have sauce? No. Then I checked the fridge. Breakfast dinner was usually a staple. Did I have eggs? No. Into the cupboard. Peanut butter and jelly? No. Tomato soup? Nope.

The dogs barked.

"SHUT UP!" all three kids screamed in unison.

The dogs stopped barking. Triston hammered on the piano.

I tried to think of various combinations for dinner. Why was this suddenly so hard? An impossible algebra equation I could not solve, as I was missing at least one key ingredient. Butter. It all came back to butter. I could not do anything, it seemed, without butter. What kind of decent mother of three kids does not have butter?

I remember the feeling of the floor giving out. Like the ground wanted to swallow me but decided against it and spit me out. I could not breathe. I gasped for air.

"Bb…bbbbb…butter." Everything went black as I crumpled to the ground, my face against the dirty floor.

The piano went silent. The kids appeared over me one by one and looked nervous. "Is she okay?" my daughter said.

"I'm sorry, I don't know what to make for dinner," I sobbed. "We…have…no…bbbutter."

Prior to this moment, I believed if I tried hard enough, I could figure things out. But I had woken up to a bad marriage, I was using alcohol to numb my pain, and the overweight woman in the mirror with dull, sad eyes and blotchy skin was not the person I wanted to be. I could not even look at her.

People talk about hitting bottom.

And I did.

I was lucky. Failure is a gift. Rock bottom gives you few options. So, I chose to go up.

Then, so many amazing things happened. It took years, but I slowly put my life back together. Gratitude became the key to a positive mindset and the path to a better, happier life. Day by day, I worked to build the life I wanted. I went back to college, met the man I love (and married), committed to improving myself while raising a family, and built wealth.

I now start each day with gratitude and have learned positive mindset is the key to happiness. In fact, there is new emerging science on gratitude as a habit and how it can make you feel happier and healthier.

Gratitude can be described as: identifying what we are grateful for and giving thanks for what we have; also known in positive psychology as the human way of acknowledging the good things in life (Emmons 2013). Some recent studies show gratitude has many benefits including increased happiness, higher life satisfaction, better physical health, more restful sleep, lower levels of anxiety and/or depression, and less burnout.

In this book, I explore the science of gratitude as well as its many benefits. I interview experts in positive mindset and psychology, and show research from leading scientists studying this movement, as well as others who have used gratitude to get through tough times or trauma.

Together, we will explore a map of gratitude and how to cultivate a daily practice to improve your mood, your health, and your life with step-by-step instructions using the *Four Habits of Grateful*.

This book is also a collection of stories. A reflection of my personal journey, from bad to good to just WOW. As a female leader, real estate industry expert, mom, friend, wife, and, most of all, a student of gratitude, I have learned our greatest desire is to feel appreciated and loved: *that we matter.* In the boardroom, the kitchen, or on the sidewalk, this is the common thread binding us all.

I am grateful for being alive and for being here right now. I am grateful I am healthy. I can see. I can hear. I can breathe. I have a beautiful home that is warm with plentiful food and nice clothes. A walk-in closet. Marble floors. But most importantly, I am grateful for my children and the love we share. I am grateful for my husband; he is my best friend.

Around every corner is a new and wonderful surprise. A kind smile, a new friend, a mentor, or someone to whom I can lend a hand. The sun is shining and everywhere I look, there are miracles of blue sky, water, flowers in bloom, the stars, and the night sky. A brilliant sunset.

I am grateful for the many friends and family members that have helped me on my journey. They are the most beautiful and precious things in life.

You see, once I had nothing and was drowning.

Today, I have everything.

What Is Gratitude?

"If we do not feel grateful for what we
already have, what makes us think we'd be
happy with more?"

—UNKNOWN

Gratitude is a buzzword. Listen for it and you will hear it every-where. In conversations, in the boardroom, on social media, and in the pages of books by Brené Brown, Glennon Doyle, and Simon Sinek. "I appreciate you" is something you might be told; the words softly lobbed from a stranger like a COVID-19 safe hug in Starbucks.

But being grateful is more than a buzzword. What if gratitude could help you feel better (mentally and physically), strengthen your relationships, and help you feel balanced? What if you discovered gratitude is a superpower you already possess? You just need to start using it.

It is easy to get snarky, eye roll, and dismiss the public #blessed overtures on social media. Gratitude might appear in your Instagram feed or perhaps #thankful as an influencer boards a private jet or enjoys a vegan dinner for two on the terrace of a castle in the Alps. You have probably seen this public show of thanks like a disclaimer for those who seem to have it all: #grateful. After all, isn't it easier to be grateful when your "cup runneth over"?

My sister, Dr. Kim, a longtime therapist and now a PhD, has studied psychology and social work for many years. I called her on a Sunday for one of our normal sister-to-sister conversations ranging from what our kids are eating/playing to what outfit we are wearing.

I said, "I think I discovered something. It's called 'gratitude' and it is changing my life!" I then elaborated and went into more detail.

She laughed, "Yes. That is called positive psychology. We use that in therapy as a coping mechanism. It's pretty mainstream in my world."

Why had we never talked about it?

It seemed the deeper I dug into gratitude, the more I found it everywhere. Lurking. I found myself wondering: **What exactly is gratitude?**

"The definition of gratitude, which rhymes with 'attitude,' comes from the Latin word gratus, which means 'thankful, pleasing.'"

A google search of what is gratitude:

- A positive emotion
- Being thankful
- Showing appreciation
- An affirmation of goodness
- A personality trait, mood, or emotion
- A core component of many religions
- You are grateful for what you have
- A positive emotional reaction
- A mental state of mind
- A warm feeling
- A choice

But the gratitude I researched was not a one-night stand. Not just Thanksgiving every November or a thank you card you write after a birthday gift. Instead, my definition of gratitude is a daily practice of thoughts and actions, a new way of looking at everything in your orbit. Almost like meditation but, well, different. If you think about daily habits like showering, exercise, brushing your teeth, etc., gratitude should be one of them. Daily focus defined by actions. Not just a mindset but a way of life.

I learned very quickly there are others like me who practice gratitude daily. In fact, the more I began talking about it the more they came out of the woodwork like an underground cult. Those who practice gratitude are the happiest, most well-rounded people I know. They are upbeat. There is a spring in their step. You might say their eyes even sparkle. They seem to have more joy than others. At times it is contagious. But how to define this trait? This superpower?

Fast forward to 2021. COVID-19 is a dark, wet blanket over the world. We are united in trauma and lockdowns. Anger and fear are rampant. And yet gratitude seems to be ever present, right in the corners if you look close enough. On bookshelves. Is there a craving to feel more united amidst the gloom and doom? To appreciate? When we are stripped of our most basic needs, we are suddenly reminded of what we once had. There is a natural response to look back.

And in times of war or destruction, in death and loss, we as humans tend to band together tighter than before. COVID-19 made us more appreciative of all we took for granted. It created a shift. But again, this is reactionary. What about daily intentional gratitude? The kind you practice even when you have everything?

There is emerging research. Hundreds of science-based studies and evidence suggest a habit of grateful can make people feel happier. A stronger immune system. Better mental health and less depression (Allen 2018).

In an article, Dr. Robert Emmons, "the world's leading scientific expert on gratitude" says gratitude makes us happier and healthier (Emmons 2013). His widely published research indicates the benefits "systematically cultivating gratitude" will give us:

- Physical benefits: stronger immune system, less bothered by aches and pains, lower blood pressure, easier to exercise, taking better care of health, longer periods of sleep, and feeling more refreshed upon waking

- Psychological benefits: higher levels of positive emotions, more alert, alive, and awake, more joy and pleasure, more optimism and happiness

- Social benefits: more helpful, generous, and compassionate, more forgiving, more outgoing, less feelings of loneliness and isolation

Clearly, Emmons identifies a practice or habit of gratitude as having the most benefit. He also writes about "gratitude intervention," which is a way to infuse activities into your life. This can include keeping a gratitude journal, writing notes of gratitude, appreciating others throughout your day, and consciously reflecting on what you are grateful for (morning or night).

More than ever, we see connections between our thoughts and our physical body. Our thoughts can influence pathways in our brain and therefore our physical response. Clinical psychologist Madhuleena Roy Chowdhury discovered the practice of gratitude is life-altering. She says, "When we express gratitude and receive the same, our brain releases dopamine and serotonin, the two crucial neurotransmitters responsible for our emotions, and they make us feel 'good.' They enhance our mood immediately, making us feel happy from the inside" (Chowdhury 2019).

This superpower you and I both have can be activated like flipping a switch. It can generate *feel-good chemicals*. Let's face it, depression and anxiety are at all-time highs (as are liquor and drug sales). What if a habit of grateful brought you more joy and less yuck?

Can gratitude be the holy grail, the new Prozac, and the answer to everything? Even Oprah Winfrey sings the praises of gratitude. She is widely known for her quote, "Be thankful for what you have; you'll end up having more. If you concentrate on what you don't have, you will never, ever have enough." And while it's easy for someone who has everything to preach gratitude, what if one of the reasons they got there was by fully harnessing this super-power? Even Tony Robbins uses gratitude in his programs that people pay thousands of dollars to attend. Who else uses a habit of grateful, you might ask? People like Mother Teresa, Arianna Huffington, and Richard Branson. World leaders. Past presidents of the United States like Obama and Bush. Because it works.

In my worst moments, I drowned in a tidal wave of disappointment and loss. I once lived in a scarcity mindset. I did not have enough. I was angry and jealous. I knew living in a scarcity mindset was not healthy and I could not continue feeling, well, like a loser. I made a BIG change. And it worked.

How? By being grateful. I learned how to harness my super-power. A daily practice of gratitude not only helped me crawl out of the hole I was in during my divorce and financial hardship but it also changed my entire outlook on life. I am more balanced, happier, and in good health. When I am in a bad mood, I snap back easily to a positive mindset. And it just feels good.

I noticed when I consciously practiced gratitude, my entire uni-verse shifted. In fact, this daily habit helped me to get the life I once dreamed of. I learned day after day to focus on what I have and more would come. To thank those who stood beside me. To appreciate things like trees, friends, a good meal, and even small things.

Like a superhero who wakes up one day to find new powers, you can emerge recharged and happier than ever. It's amazing what you can attract when you live in a state of appreciation. A habit of grateful is waiting for you. Step into your superpower.

Ancient History I

My marriage came to an end like a sputtering car that ran out of gas. I had ignored the empty light for too long and was still surprised when it died.

I will never forget the couples counseling sessions, tucked inside an old Victorian home turned office. Outside, summer was unfolding. Cars whooshed by.

Our therapist, Phil, was a soft-spoken man in his late fifties with a gray beard and understanding brown eyes. I got the feeling he genuinely wanted to help, with a compassionate gaze and Keds sneakers.

My now ex-husband of eleven years sat next to me on the couch, his arms folded, biceps chunky and tight. A tattoo of a Japanese carp wrapped around his forearm. Every time I saw it poking out of his sleeve, I was angry.

He is the type of handsome that stops women on the street and causes them to throw themselves at him like goo, loose and sticky. But we were older now, and his looks did not impress me anymore. Instead, I saw the disappointment of a failed marriage. The shirt he is wearing I picked out and paid for. His hands folded on his lap. The fish curled against his arm, scales flexing as he breathed. Just under the surface of water, each dot a prick of a needle; purple, green, and blue.

"Dan, what are your thoughts?" Phil asked.

Dan took up more than half the couch. I was careful to maintain a foot of space so we weren't touching. He looked at Phil with the expression of a scolded child in the principal's office. "I don't know."

Dan offered his winning smile.

Phil was unaffected by the smile. In that moment I was happy we had a male marriage therapist. I had tried to be careful in the steps of dissolving our marriage; this letting go. I wanted to do it right.

"But Dan, we sat here. In this very room, months ago. Kristine made it clear things were not working."

I studied the scuffed secondhand coffee table and a poster of a kitten hanging by its claw with the words "hang in there" in an awful purple font. I wanted to leave that shabby room, with the crappy couch I sank into, drowning each time we saw Phil.

Dan sat back, like someone hit him. "I don't know. I just don't know."

I had been in this situation hundreds of times. Dan hoped for another chance. That his charm would be like the wave of a magic wand. Phil would offer some suggestions, like date night, and we would go home to our unfinished house in various stages of construction, with our three young children stacked inside, and pretend everything was fine.

It was not fine. Not even close.

At home, I was afraid to answer the door. The mailman would stand on the front porch, knock, and sheepishly hand me stacks of certified letters while trying to peek inside. Liens, judgments, and collection letters. Finally, I stopped answering the door. Then I stopped getting the mail. Eventually the mailbox started overflowing onto the street.

We were both self-employed and overextended. We got a tax bill so large I almost fainted. Our accounts were frozen by the IRS. It all came crashing down. With a final swoop of financial destruction, we were launched into IRS abyss. "Uncollectable" is what IRS Agent 35477789 told me on the phone when I called to try to set up a payment plan. We were doomed.

Phil's voice pulled me back into the room. "So, Kristine, what are you going to do?" Dan looked at me, hot tears leaking down his cheeks. I knew those tears. I had tasted those tears. I knew every pore of him.

"I want a separation," I said.

Phil didn't look surprised.

That night, we returned home in separate cars and went through our normal routine of getting the kids fed, bathed, and to bed. Our therapy was like a stench permeating the house. It was easier for us to slip back into our role as parents, on autopilot, and take care of the kids. I waited until all three of them were asleep.

Dan joined me in the living room. "I can't believe you are doing this to me. To us." I could smell whiskey on his breath.

I made myself a vodka. We were both unhappy and drank too much at night. It was no one's fault. The anger and resentment had pent up over the years and ate away at our love until there was nothing left.

I sat across from him near the fireplace. "I am sorry," I said. I was numb and tired of feeling let down each day. We had tried counseling. We tried going away on a vacation without the kids. And yet nothing worked. Things just got worse.

We started a construction project on the house and it had been half-finished for years. Tyvek flapped in the wind. More stress. More blame.

"I am sorry, but I can't do this anymore. I just can't," I said firmly.

"You don't love me?"

I didn't answer. I hadn't loved him in a long time. The car was out of gas. We needed a tow truck.

After a long night of crying and trying to talk it out, we agreed he would move into a friend's condo and we would try a separation.

The next day, we gathered the kids and sat in the den. All five of us. It was officially one of the worst moments of my life. We told them the news. "We will always be a family," I said. It made me sick to say the word divorce. They were shocked.

Divorce. They knew other kids with it. The divorce word had been a creepy stranger we did not let inside our house until now.

The kids cried. Dan did too, but I wouldn't let myself. I was numb, but I wanted to appear strong. I needed to be their rock. The overwhelming guilt of the divorce was a tight jacket on my shoulders. It confined my movements and constantly reminded me this was a choice. My choice. I was to blame.

Nights were tough. There had just been a violent home invasion in Cheshire and it was all over the news. I was still sleeping in the den on a pull-out from Ikea. Nights consisted of my five-year-old daughter next to me, and a knife under the mattress, and two phones by my side. The slightest noise woke me, so I tried sleeping with the TV on.

The dynamic of the house changed without a man. Even the dogs seemed more rambunctious, and I realized it was the alpha male they were missing. I resolved to grow balls, speak louder, and stand straight.

Outside in the driveway, motion lights flashed on and off like a continuous lightning storm. Everything woke me. An owl. A creak. A clank. Three a.m. was an old college friend returned after ten years.

It took me weeks before I could sleep without my bedside lamp on or the glow and chatter of television. Thankfully, the Olympics were on all hours of the night. I watched athletes jumping, sweating, and competing at two in the morning. It was oddly comforting.

After two weeks, I hit a crossroad. My five-year-old cried, "Why doesn't Daddy live here?" She asked when he would come back. To *sleep* home. It seemed everyone was, in fact, obsessed with sleep.

I calmly explained Daddy lived at his condo now.

"Forever?" she asked, pleading for me to say no. She even shook her head. *Say no.*

"Yes, from now on. You will stay here with Mommy and you will stay with Daddy too. Both of us, forever."

She was five. This did not make any sense. She sucked her thumb, tired. She didn't understand the condo. It didn't have a yard.

I tucked her in, drying tears. I rubbed her soft blonde hair.

"Goodnight, baby," I said. I stayed with her until she fell asleep.

Later that night, I wandered around the house. It looked different. I was suddenly responsible for every little thing in the household, from dishes to cleaning up dog poop, to grocery shopping and laundry. It was exhausting.

As I loaded the dishwasher, I was suddenly greeted by a squeaking field mouse. I screamed and ran into the living room, grabbed a blanket, and threw it over my head. What in the world would I do? I had set a chain of events into motion that could not be stopped. Like the game Mouse Trap. How fitting. How would I do this?

Have you ever felt all alone? Scared?

A mindset of scarcity or a "victim mindset" is a dark, scary forest. It is easy to let the dark forest grow so big it can choke out the sunlight. In fact, so much darkness can convince you things will never get better and you will never find a way out. Unless, of course, you find breadcrumbs.

Breadcrumbs are a trail of hope; the path used by others to escape the dark forest.

Writer Elizabeth Gilbert created an Instagram post in 2019 on her account with what she calls a "Gratitude Bomb." She instructs: Draw a sun (small circle) in the middle of a piece of paper or your journal. Then draw lines going out from the sun all around it. Then, on each ray of sunlight, write something you are grateful for. Gilbert says, "Let the words spill right off the page, with the understanding that this galaxy is expanding. Imagine that your gratitude is shooting right out into space" (Gilbert 2019).

Can you draw a Gratitude Bomb right now? Can you pause and take a moment and draw the sun with rays of all the things you are grateful for?

It's amazing what the warm sun of gratitude will do for you. It turns out a Gratitude Bomb can chase away the darkness, scary monsters, and even help you find your way out of a dark forest. Breadcrumbs. Follow the breadcrumbs.

A Gratitude Bomb will not, however, remove a mouse from your kitchen sink. It turns out that requires a different superpower of which I have yet to master.

What Does Gratitude Mean to You?

The thing about anxiety is it creeps up on you. It is undefinable. I wish I could paint it with words; define it with color and shape. But the worst part of fear is that it has no shape. It is everywhere. It is the unknown. The invisible shape of *bad*. A thousand tiny spikes of ice against your soul.

Have you ever suffered from feelings of anxiety and/or depression? Have you ever wondered, How can I feel less anxious and/or depressed without drugs or alcohol to numb the pain?

Do you desire to be more balanced in your emotions?

According to the APA's 2021 Stress in America Survey, the COVID-19 pandemic has taken a toll on Generation Z's mental health (Akers 2022):

- Thirty-seven percent of Gen Z adults report being so stressed about the pandemic that they struggle to make basic decisions; 50 percent struggle to make major life decisions (however, Millennials had an even more difficult time with decision-making).

- Seventy-nine percent report experiencing behavior changes due to stress.

- Nearly half (45 percent) of the Gen Z survey respondents report they do not know how to manage their pandemic-related stress.

When I was engulfed in my pending divorce and facing a tsunami of financial ruin, my level of anxiety was at an all-time high. I felt hopeless. I had moments of full-blown panic. Every fiber inside me ached and burned at the same time and I could hear my pulse clattering around my temples. Adrenaline pumped through me. I asked myself, *Am I dying?* Things were cloudy. I grabbed onto whatever I could find to steady myself. A counter. A chair. Then it would finally pass.

I got stronger. Better at this new thing called "being alone" when the kids were at their dad's house every other weekend. When they came back on Sunday, I hugged them even tighter. Being a mother is one of my greatest gifts. When I consciously think of my children and really focus on being grateful for them, it's like a warm bright light of love. It melts away the fear. I call it a "heart melt."

Most of us love Thanksgiving because the focus is sitting around a table and being grateful for food, family, and friends. It's fun to go around the table and ask everyone, "What are you grateful for?"

I recently posted a survey on Facebook and asked, **"What does gratitude mean to you?"**

Here are the responses (which are lovely):

- A reminder that I have a wonderful life and appreciate it. Easy to take for granted.

- Gratitude is a vibration inside of me that helps me put my mind in a space that allows me to serve others and better myself.

- A sense that there is an abundance of good things in the world when we remind ourselves to look for it. Especially when we feel like something is lacking.

- Remembering how lucky you are to be at this point in your life.

- Gratitude is positivity. It means to appreciate every day.

- Stopping daily with my hands open, not a tight fist.

- It's a thank you to the universe or whatever your faith may be.

- It means being content even in the midst of difficulty.

- Recognizing my blessings despite everything going on around me.

- Peace and perspective.

- Gratitude creates happiness, helps deal with adversity, improves relationships.

o Identify anything that creates joy and abundance and fills my heart with happiness.

o Pausing and recognizing what I do have rather than the wants.

o It means to recognize both the small and the large blessings in your life.

o Gratitude is everything to me. Without gratitude we are empty and broke.

o Control of my thinking; choosing to be happy for all I have.

o Identifying gratitude helps keep it at the forefront of our consciousness, which will in turn have positive effects on our attitudes, mindfulness, and overall being.

o It's win-win; good for me and leads to goodness for those around me.

o Everything.

VISUALIZATION EXERCISE

Imagine you are at the Thanksgiving table of your choice. Who is sitting at that table? It can be anyone: someone alive or someone who has passed. Imagine yourself sitting at a big table piled high with all your most favorite dishes. As you look around, who is sitting there with you? Can you name them? Can you thank them for being with you?

As you imagine yourself at this Thanksgiving table, what does it feel like?

What does gratitude mean to you?

Ancient History II

"Remember that sometimes not getting what you want is a wonderful stroke
of luck."

—DALAI LAMA

Pay attention to the people you surround yourself with. They
become the soundtrack of your life. Surround yourself with positive people. Good people who lift you up and help you succeed.

Distance yourself from the negative ones. The haters. The ones
who tell you you can't do it or that you will never get ahead. The
saying "misery loves company" is true. Protect yourself.

After my ex-husband moved out, things got tough. We were
suddenly in a new world with new rules. Co-parenting. Visi-
tation. Awkward custody exchanges. Each day was a struggle.

Thankfully, my family and friends rallied around me. Without
them I don't know where I would be today. But you don't need
an army. In life, all you need are a few good people. Even one.

I was in a funk. I did not want to see anyone or go anywhere. I was feeling depressed and shamed about the separation. In the grocery store, other moms stopped me and asked, "Are you okay?" Others just gave me "stank eye" as they stacked up on Tide and Downy. A small town gets even smaller when divorce goes public.

My friend, Mary, invited the kids and I to a sunset picnic. She belonged to a private club. Mary was one of the greatest gifts during the impending divorce. We had enjoyed a long friendship and her eyes sparkled with a joy for life that was contagious. She was older with beautiful blue eyes and short gray hair. Big earrings. Big smile. One of those people you meet and instantly like.

"I don't think we can go," I said, trying to think of an excuse. I was embarrassed and did not want to talk to anyone.

"It will be good for you. Plus, the kids will love the lake," she said. "Think about it."

She was right. I would do it for the kids. "Okay. Thanks for the invite. We will be there."

The next day I struggled to get the kids ready. They each disappeared to the corners of the house: Triston in his room playing Nintendo, Jacob building Legos in the den, and Amelia, my little shadow, following me around as I gathered towels.

"Let's go, in the car," I yelled. Finally, we all piled in.

We got to the lake around five o'clock and there was a cool breeze. The silver water was a mirror of sky and clouds. We enjoyed a wonderful picnic of pasta salad and mini sandwiches with some fresh fruit cut into cubes.

Mary and I sat on white wooden chairs and watched the kids swim. Amelia ran along the sand and looked for things to put in her bucket. She had just turned five and would start kindergarten in the fall. Her blond hair and bright blue eyes always melted my heart. The boys took turns diving underwater. She waded in and floated on her back. For a moment, I forgot all the bad stuff happening in my life.

Then a wave of nausea hit me. I could pretend this was just a normal outing. I was a normal mom with three kids at the lake. But that was a lie, like most of my life now. The edges had already cracked; they were getting deeper and deeper.

"Are you okay?" Mary asked. "You look sad."

"I don't know how I am going to do this," I said. "I am terrified." Tears streamed down my face. I wiped them away quickly so the kids would not see.

She inched closer to me and grabbed my hand. "Kristine, you can do this. You will get through it."

Her words gave me strength.

She looked me in the eyes and said, "You are strong. And you are kind. You are smart. And you are beautiful, inside and out." I looked away, uncomfortable. I did not feel any of those things.

"You are working hard and you can do this. I know you can," she said firmly.

"Thank you," I squeezed her hand.

It's hard to describe the exact feeling when someone else believes in you and they see a strength, even when you don't see it. Her words lent me courage. Her kindness made me feel worthy. We sat in silence.

I watched the three kids play and the sun began to sink into the horizon. Beautiful colors of orange and yellow filled the sky and we watched it like a painting. It made me sad.

I have always loved sunsets, even if that night felt unsettled. Lonely. What would it be like to enjoy a sunset with ease? To not have this feeling of foreboding hanging over me?

"I am so happy you came tonight. This was a gift," Mary said.

In that moment I was grateful for my friend Mary. Grateful to be a mom.

"Let's go get ice cream," Mary suggested as we packed up our beach things. "Peaches and Cream?"

"Yay!" the kids cheered.

I felt the weight of guilt again. I did not have money for ice cream. "Um, we have stuff at home," I said.

The kids groaned. "We don't want popsicles, Mom. Please?"

"My treat," Mary said.

"I can't let you do that, you already—"

"It is my treat, Kristine!" she said. "I don't want to go all alone and you know how much I love ice cream," she insisted.

"Okay. I guess we can go. Thank you." The kids cheered.

We drove to Peaches and Cream. When Mary paid, I felt awkward and looked away. "Thank you so much," I said. The kids dug into their cones.

In that moment, I felt inadequate. I did not want to come across as a beggar or charity case. But then Mary winked at me. "This ice cream, isn't it *heaven?*" she giggled.

Amelia sat down next to her and laughed.

It took me many years to understand there is a cycle to giving. It turns out to complete the cycle, you have to be open to receiving. You see, by allowing Mary to treat us to ice cream and give us a kindness, I learned how to receive her kindness without shame and say thank you.

Have you ever had a friend who was there for you when you needed it most? Someone who believed in you? Someone who constantly tried to lift you with kind words and love?

If you have ever flown a kite, then you know that moment when the wind catches it and suddenly lifts the kite into the air. That is what really good friendship is: when a friend lifts you up. A force. When there is a mutual feeling of gratitude. Of love.

In his blog, *The Daily Motivator*, Ralph Marston writes, "In ways you do not even realize, life is thankful for you. And as you continue to return that gratitude, goodness expands in every direction" (Marston 2021). Remember to express your appreciation sincerely and without the expectation of anything in return.

The next day, I wrote Mary a note. I told her how much her friendship meant to me. I thanked her for the ice cream, but most importantly, for being my friend. Expressing my gratitude felt like a way I could honor her and give back kindness. It felt so good to send the note. And when she received it, I imagined she felt the cycle of giving full circle. We wrote letters throughout our friendship. Each one was a gift.

A few months later I filed for divorce. I will never forget the feeling of putting the paperwork in the mailbox. Divorce was the hardest thing I ever did. I recognize it was a choice, and it's a heavy choice. With it comes ripples of pain, and it touches every part of your kids' lives and their future.

The fear was there. Nipping at my ankles.

I am a failure.
I am breaking up my family.
I can't do this alone.
I am selfish.

A friend once told me divorce is like walking through fire: the only way through the pain is to walk through it. Then get on the other side of the hurt and heal.

Others have compared it to jumping off a cliff.

Either way, I knew it would hurt.

All of us.

Not Today

Run.

She pushed the side door open hard and heard it smack against the house. BOOM.

She didn't care. Nothing mattered.

The pain leaked out of her and came up like bile. She couldn't breathe. She gasped for air beneath the primal sobs that shook her body. Snot leaked down her face.

She ran to the river at the back of the property, needing to flee to the edges of her life.

Slippers. She had on slippers in the snow. They were soaked.

Breathe. Just breathe.

The kids were all at school. She was alone.

The river was chunked up with blocks of ice and snow. Soapy green under the surface, the current stronger than usual as it pushed and nudged the ice.

The pressure. Something had to give.

How deep was the water?

I can't...I just can't anymore.

She thought about throwing herself into the river and letting go. This was the second time she'd had such thoughts. Last week, she had fantasied about driving into oncoming traffic. One turn of the wheel and it could be over.

The pain. Gone.

She was weak. She could not do this anymore. She cried.

Gasping...in and out...

Her eyes were raw. They burned.

Everything hurt.

Then a calming inside. So this is what it was like. To give up.

The sobs subsided.

Exhaustion.

Her feet were numb.

She knew her children needed her.

She had to be strong. For them.

And so she chose to live.

Not today. I won't give up today.

She walked back to the broken house, her head down in shame, her slippers ruined.

If you are reading this and have ever felt like this, I want you to know you are not alone.

Keep going.

Positive Mindset

Are you happy because you are successful or successful because you are happy?

I stumbled upon Shawn Achor because of his TED talk, "The Happy Secret to Better Work." It is one of the funniest and most compelling TED talks I have ever watched. Turns out he is a Harvard professor, researcher, author, and one of the world's leading experts on the connection between happiness and success. In his book *The Happiness Advantage*, Achor writes, "When we are happy—when our mindset and mood are positive—we are smarter, more motivated, and thus more successful. Happiness is the center, and success revolves around it" (Achor 2018).

Achor recognizes gratitude is one of the easiest ways to develop a positive mindset. I wish I had his book with me a few weeks ago when I was at the nail salon. I would have handed it to the two young ladies chatting loud enough everyone could hear their conversation.

"Each day I wake up and hear so many negative voices in my head." She had on jeans and a black T-shirt and a tattoo on her wrist. She slumped in her chair.

Her friend, also young and pretty, nodded in agreement. "Me too. I always feel depressed."

They continued to talk about anxiety and panic attacks. The first one added, "I want to try and be more positive, but it is so hard."

It saddened me to hear two young women so consumed by stress and anxiety. But I was not surprised. This seems rampant. I am not sure if it is caused by endless technology or if it's just more mainstream to acknowledge anxiety and talk about it openly.

So, what are some ways to help manage our anxiety? Is gratitude the answer?

TRY ON SOME GRATITUDE

In my interview with Sue Sidway, a licensed family therapist, she said, "For most people, they are more attuned to the negative things that are happening. It takes attention and habit learning in order to reverse that negativity bias." This is where we need to be careful. Stop noticing the negative things. Stop giving them your energy.

Ask yourself, are you constantly focused only on the negative? All of the things you don't have?

I just want to clarify that anxiety and depression are serious and gratitude is just one tool that can help combat them. Getting help from a licensed therapist or doctor is crucial, especially if you are having life-threatening feelings or if you can't function. Help is always available. You just have to ask for it. Prioritize mental health treatment with a professional should you find yourself chronically depressed or having bad thoughts.

The more you focus on what you don't want, the more energy you give to a negative bias. When we focus on gratitude, we illuminate all the positive. Life is like a television, and guess what? YOU can change the channel on your TV. You have the remote control in your hand and you control what channel you are watching. So, what will it be?

When one commits to a daily habit of gratitude (in good times and bad), there are many benefits. By consciously focusing on being grateful every day and using a method to apply gratitude to your life, you will see that life gets better, more colorful, and your relationships with others deepen. Your state of being will be enriched. You won't lose your temper as much and you won't covet things as much. You will feel happier.

This does not mean you won't find yourself in a bad mood occasionally. You will still feel depressed sometimes because, let's face it, we are all human. In fact, I was in a bad mood last week, but I rarely have these ugly moments since I have been practicing gratitude daily. I can switch into a positive mindset with ease. The more you practice gratitude as a habit, the easier you can harness it when needed.

I recently got a facial and my esthetician, Andrea, and I got on the topic of gratitude. She shared, "My husband and I have been purchasing meals from a wonderful meal prep delivery service since we had our daughter. It is such a help because we both work and want to eat clean. They arrive at our door in a special cooler. The guy, Steve, that delivers them is really nice.

He always texts me to make sure the cooler is out and that it has ice in it. He goes above and beyond.

If I am home, he brings them inside into our fridge and is really nice. He is partly deaf and has trouble communicating. But he is kind and considerate. I realized after a few deliveries we had not tipped him. I decided to give him an extra big tip and along with it I wrote a note telling him how much I appreciated how he was always so considerate in his delivery times, and just so nice. I didn't think much of it, I just wanted to do a kindness for him. Well, the owner of the company called to personally thank me. He said Steve the delivery guy got my note and it meant so much to him that he cried. The owner then said, 'Steve *never* cries.'"

One of the best parts of gratitude is it takes focus off yourself and causes you to be external. This helps with anxiety and depression because you redirect your thoughts from yourself to others. If you can make others feel good and appreciated, you will in fact feel better. The more you focus on gratitude, the more meaningful your relationships will be.

There is also evidence that a grateful disposition is associated with life satisfaction, optimism, subjective well-being, positive affect, and happiness. Because, really, what is the alternative? To have a negative disposition means to be dark in thought and only see the negative. That is not a fun place to live. And let's face it, some of us must work harder at being grateful than others. That's okay. In time, with daily habits of gratitude, you can change the way you see the world.

Tony Robbins calls it an abundance mindset. The *Tony Robbins Blog* states, "The belief that there are enough resources in the world for everyone—and of being grateful for whatever the universe provides. It's often talked about in contrast with a scarcity mindset, or the belief that the world's resources are finite" (Team Tony 2022).

We can shift our perspective into an abundance mindset by appreciating others, giving back, and living in the present. Robbins also cautions against "self-limiting beliefs" and recommends making a list of all you are grateful for. This will focus your mindset onto abundance. All the gifts and blessings you have (Team Tony 2022).

THE SCIENCE OF GRATITUDE

"You will find that many of the truths we cling to depend greatly on our own point of view."
—OBI-WAN KENOBI, *RETURN OF THE JEDI* (2013).

Consider the following:

In a 2008 study, "The Neural Basis of Human Social Values: Evidence from Functional MRI," researchers measured brain activity of participants experiencing different emotions and found gratitude causes synchronized activation in multiple brain regions and lights up parts of the brain's reward pathways and the hypothalamus (Zahn 2008). When we release gratitude and receive the same, our brain releases dopamine and serotonin, two crucial neurotransmitters responsible for our emotions. They make us feel good and enhance our mood.

A handful of neuroimaging studies have shed light on brain areas likely involved in experiencing and expressing gratitude. One functional magnetic resonance imaging (fMRI) study found experiencing emotions involved in maintaining social values, such as pride and gratitude, activated areas in the meso-limbic and basal forebrain, regions involved in feelings of reward and the formation of social bonds (Zahn 2009).

A follow-up study found people who more readily experience gratitude have more gray matter in their right inferior temporal cortex, an area previously linked to interpreting other people's intentions (Zahn, Garrido, Moll, and Grafman, 2014).

Gratitude is associated with other positive traits and disposi-tions, such as agreeableness (McCullough 2002), forgivingness, patience, happiness, and hope (Witvliet et al. 2018). Like other positive emotions, gratitude broadens the scope of one's cogni-tion and behaviors, which allows for developing more psycho-logical and social resources (Fredrickson 2013).

There is a plethora of scientific research on gratitude and the brain that suggests physical benefits of mindfulness. More than enough evidence to merit a practice of gratitude. But beyond science and data, pay attention to how you *feel* when you practice gratitude. Is it calming? Peaceful? Does it soothe?

You may ask, what does a habit of gratitude look like? I am happy to share it's not that hard. The easiest way to begin is to follow the Four Habits of Grateful as outlined in this book.

Are you ready to change your life?

Let's explore this process in more detail.

The Habits of Grateful: Daily Mindset

Gratitude practiced as a habit can make you feel happier and healthier. There are many ways to start using gratitude to improve your life. When practiced regularly, good habits can help you have a positive mindset and embrace gratitude.

THE HABIT OF GRATEFUL #1—DAILY GRATITUDE

- Upon waking, ask yourself, *What am I grateful for today?*

- List three things you are grateful for.

- You can say them aloud, to yourself (internally), or write them down in a journal.

HABIT #2—BE THE SUNSHINE

- Look for opportunities to appreciate others throughout your day.

- Tell everyone you meet in person you "appreciate them."

- Perform acts of kindness to inspire others.

- Use the words "I appreciate you" in conversation.

HABIT #3—WRITING NOTES OF GRATITUDE

- Write handwritten notes of gratitude and send them in the mail.

- Aim for five to seven a week, or more if you wish.

- Tell others why you are grateful for them.

- Use the enclosed writing prompts.

HABIT # 4—COMMIT

- Vitamin G: take your gratitude pill every day.

- Make gratitude a morning/evening habit.

- Track your progress.

- Sign a Gratitude Contract.

(BONUS) GRATITUDE INTERVENTION

If you want to supercharge your habit of grateful, a Gratitude Intervention is an intense way to jump in. The following are activities with a strong focus on gratitude for thirty days:

- Morning and evening gratitude

- Stickies on mirrors that say, "I am grateful for ___."

- Affirmations of gratitude

- Gratitude notepad/journal

- One note a day to others

- Tell strangers you meet (barista, waiter, mailman, or delivery person) you appreciate them

- Random acts of kindness to spread gratitude

- Tell the most important people in your life you are thankful for them and why in a letter or in person.

Dig

A financial and economic hurricane was brewing just offshore. Would it make landfall?

Over the past eight years, I earned a great living as a real estate agent. I built a team, rented office space, and established myself in the community. I was climbing a ladder of success and relished not only the surge in income but also the understanding that I could keep increasing my business. I took on more overhead.

Then the economy changed entirely. It was 2008. As *Investopedia* described it:

The worst crisis in nearly eight decades engulfed the global financial system, bringing Wall Street's giants to their knees and triggering the Great Recession. It was an epic financial and economic collapse that cost many ordinary people their jobs, their life savings, their homes, or all three. (Singh 2022)

Everything contracted.

Earlier that year, one of the highlights of my career was a nineteen-million-dollar castle in Great Barrington, Massachusetts. I worked in a market where the average home sold for 400k. The magnitude of listing a castle for sale was unlike anything I had ever encountered. For months I researched and catalogued the history of the Searles Castle and compiled notes and drawings of each room and all the different stone, wood, and materials. The listing launched and I will never forget it. It was on the AP news ticker. A huge splash. Tons of PR.

We eventually inked a sales contract. I added up the potential commission. It would be life-changing. We could finish the renovations on our house. We would pay off our debt. This would save us. Everything would change. Like any superstitious real estate agent, I logged the closing date on my calendar in pencil. I said prayers. And I waited.

A few weeks before the closing, the owner called me. I pulled over to take his call. I will never forget where I was that day: parked in downtown Litchfield looking up at the old stone courthouse.

He said the words that would change the course of the storm. It now would make landfall.

"The deal is off. I am keeping the deposit."

Category Five.

My mind raced and I grasped the steering wheel of my car. Could we fix it? Could we save the deal?

"The deal is dead," he said again.

Panic set in. I had counted on this huge commission. Now what?

The financial crash of 2008 affected many in real estate. Suddenly my phone stopped ringing. My pending deals toppled like dominoes. My entire pipeline of income was gone.

On top of that, our family had endured its own storm. Every other Friday I helped the kids pack to go stay with their dad. The three kids all felt differently about leaving, depending on the week.

"But I want to stay *here*," Jacob said.

"I am not going!" Amelia yelled.

"When will Dad get here?" Triston asked, looking out the front window. "I want to stay with him."

We divided the kids like dissecting them, carving out separate lives in separate houses. I wondered about what they did when they were with him. In their new house with new beds and sheets and toys and bathrooms. All their lives, I had picked out everything from their toothbrush to their snacks; and now suddenly, they had an entire universe without me, every other weekend. My heart ached.

Beep beep. The sound of their dad in the driveway. One by one they hugged me goodbye. It was like my heart had legs and left my body as they walked out of the house.

Then silence.

Overwhelming silence.

Cereal bowls in the sink. A tiny sweatshirt on the banister.

When you are a parent of three children, as amazing and beautiful as it is, it can be overwhelming. Let's be real: there are messes, food stains, temper tantrums, and in the early years, countless amounts of shit (said with love). It's easy to lose your cool or get sad, or sometimes want to raise a flag and surrender. I still remember cleaning up various textures of vomit when the stomach bug hit our house, or changing the sheets at two in the morning after a bed wetting, or nursing a child through a feverish night, or rushing one to the hospital.

To the moms and dads, I applaud you for being a parent. It is selfless. It is twenty-four seven. It requires you to put the needs of your child first and have endless patience. It is also the most beautiful and rewarding thing in life. I am incredibly lucky to be a mother. Above all, I am a mom first. Everything else is secondary.

Some divorced parents fantasize about having the house to themselves; for me, it was a jolt of pain. Suddenly, my kids were gone. Even though I knew it was temporary, it was eerie. And god, I missed them! I missed the cranky parts, the messy parts, and all the parts. I was lost.

Gratitude emerged like a beacon. Even though I faced certain financial ruin, even though we were going through a painful divorce, I was still a mother. My kids gave me purpose. I knew I was so *lucky*.

When they came back on Sunday night, I was energized with excitement. I was refreshed. I had a new perspective of what it is like to not have your kids around you. It is torture. Things like siblings fighting, throwing food, or talking back, those things became less heavy because I knew my kids, and the time I had with them, were a gift.

"How are you doing with the divorce?" Moms in the grocery store asked me.

"Do you want the real answer?" I offered, depending on how well we knew each other.

My friend Jen called me and invited me to join her for a workout or a walk. Mostly she just listened. I was lucky to have a handful of friends who urged me on.

"Have you tried Match.com?" My friend Kristen asked. "You need to get yourself back out there."

I sighed. "Eventually."

Summer turned to fall and the reality of my financial situation was like a cloud of angry bats beating against the windows of our house. How would I pay for heating oil? The last time I went to the grocery store my debit card was declined. It was humiliating. Another real estate deal fell through. Just when I thought things were better, that I could see my way out of the black hole, things got much, much worse.

My parents bought groceries for me. Money was tight. I could not get any real estate deals to close. We were still in divorce mediation, and child support had not started yet. Deferments were coming due. I was drowning.

"Mom, we are out of hot water" became a common phrase. I showered at the gym to conserve oil. I had prepaid my membership and still had a few months. I tried to navigate a payment program with the oil company and started racking up credit card debt. We had to eliminate luxuries like piano lessons, and it was amazing how quickly the bills piled up when my business took yet another nosedive.

Shortly after the butter incident, I was on the phone with my sister. "I can't seem to get a deal to close. I am not making an income."

"You need to get food stamps."

"What?"

"Food stamps. Government assistance. To buy groceries."

"Isn't that for poor people?" I asked.

Silence.

"Oh god. Am I poor?" The word *failure* loomed large in my head.

"Kris, here's the thing. Food stamps exist for times like this. You have worked and paid taxes your entire life. You are a single mom with three kids who needs groceries. There is nothing wrong with getting help. It's just short-term until you get back on your feet."

Icy fear poked my temples. I felt sick. The thought of public welfare left me feeling even more inadequate.

"Just think about it."

"If I can just close a few deals. If I can just get through my divorce…" My head ached.

"Just think, if you had some extra help each week, you could grocery shop again. Like really grocery shop. A full cart."

Wow. Fresh produce. What a thought. I was already going to Price Rite, where they charged you twenty-five cents for the grocery cart and you had to bring your own bags. It was a discount store, and everything was cheap. You never knew what you would find: sometimes the fruit was a little bruised, but your dollar went a lot further. I had given up organic years ago. Who could afford to pay three dollars for an apple?

"I will think about it." I rubbed my forehead. It was overwhelming.

A few weeks later, things got worse and I found myself in front of the social services building. I sat in my car in the parking lot, not wanting to go inside.

"I can't believe I'm here," I said to myself.

I filled out some paperwork and waited in the nondescript lobby. I shivered. Would they report me to child welfare? Would my name be on some government list of "losers"? Did I really belong here? I clutched the edges of the hard plastic chair like it might tip over. The tile was a horrible yellow. It smelled like bleach.

I had already borrowed money from my parents and a friend. I knew eventually I could sell the house; I still had equity. I hated the thought of moving the kids out of their family home.

The other day, two guys came with a trailer to tow my ex's truck. It was being repossessed. "Ma'am, do you have a key?" one asked.

"I am sorry, I don't. It belongs to my soon-to-be ex-husband. He doesn't live here anymore."

"Ma'am, if you don't give us a key, we will need to charge you an additional seven hundred dollars."

"It's not my truck."

"Can we speak to your husband?" the burly one said in an annoyed tone, clearly not believing me. "Is he inside?"

The neighbors probably watched as they loaded the truck and took it away.

I had always worked hard at real estate, nights and weekends, and made a great living. But the crash was in full swing, knocking down deals like a big crane demolishing everything in sight. Things were getting scary fast.

"Ma'am, you will be called shortly." I snapped back to reality in the waiting room. A nice elderly woman took my clipboard.

"Thanks," I said. I needed to do this for the kids. It would be temporary. I heard a door open every few minutes and they called a name.

"Kristine?" I grabbed my purse and looked up.

A gorgeous, tall guy stood in the doorway with dark blond hair.

A hot guy. Really?

I sat dumbfounded.

"Kristine?" he said again, looking around the waiting room.

I expected an older woman in polyester. Or an elderly gentleman with thick glasses and big eyebrows. I was not expecting a hot guy at social services.

"Hi. That's me," I said, totally embarrassed. I had not even bothered to put on mascara.

"Great, you can come with me and we'll go over your application."

He had nice broad shoulders. Like a superhero out of costume.

I followed him to a desk and he reviewed my application. We went over my assets (or lack thereof) and the mess of my finances. I wanted to hide. "The market has been tough. And my divorce."

"It says you have kids?"

"Three."

"Wow." He looked at me. "You seem young to have three kids."

I felt my cheeks grow hot. "Yep. And two dogs."

"Well, you obviously are a great mom if you are here getting food stamps for your kids. You'll get through this. I know it's tough, but things will get better."

"Thank you." I teared up during the appointment.

He was very kind and I could tell he had practice at lifting others he encountered. He handed me a box of tissues.

"Thank you," I said again. "I am not the type to ask for help." I wiped under my eyes, feeling self-conscious.

"Sometimes we all need help," he said.

I nodded.

"Here is your packet of information. You will get $550 a month to use for food. The cards will come to you in the mail. If you need anything, here's my information." As he handed me a packet, his nicely ironed shirt strained over toned biceps.

"Any questions?" he asked.

"No. T-t-thank you so much. This is really hard. To be h-h-here," I stuttered.

"You would be surprised at the people who come here. It's just a bit of help in the short term."

"Yes, I will only need this for a few months. Until my divorce is final."

"Good luck with that. And if you need anything, just let me know." He walked me out to the front and I was touched by his kindness. He made the process feel as undemeaning as possible.

As soon as I got into my car, I called my sister.

"How did it go?" she asked.

"Ugh. Not good. I got a hot guy."

"Really?" She sounded amused.

"Yep."

"Did you get food stamps?"

"Yes, those too. They will be coming in the mail."

"Well, even if he wanted to ask you out, you know legally he can't, right?"

"No way he'd ask me out. I'm sure he has a perfect, uncomplicated life. I have baggage. I'm damaged goods."

"Stop. I am glad you went."

"Me too. I can't wait to buy groceries!"

When the food stamp card came, it was like Christmas morning. I drove to the grocery store one town over (so I would not see people I knew in our small town) while the kids were at school and loaded up on fresh produce and meat.

The first time I used the card, people behind me rolled their eyes and I felt ashamed. Even the cashier looked me up and down. They had some issue putting it through and then finally it worked.

My face burned with humiliation, but I focused on getting help for the kids and kept telling myself this would be temporary.

That day, the bus pulled up in front of the house and the kids got off as the dogs barked.

"Hey guys, chicken with pasta for dinner. And check it out, cupcakes and ice cream sundaes tonight."

"Wow," Triston said, opening the snack cabinet.

"Cupcakes!" Jacob said.

"Yep, I made them special for you."

"Cool," Jake said, taking two. "These are mine. No one touch them," he said and brought them to his room.

Amelia and I hugged and we started her homework.

"It's nice to have a bunch of stuff in the fridge again, Mom," Triston said.

Had it gotten bad enough for him to notice? I wondered.

I had not ever appreciated things like groceries before. That night at dinner, I thought about how grateful I was to make a nice meal for the kids.

I stared at the full cabinets and said to myself:

I am grateful for food.

I am grateful for the kindness of others.

I am grateful the nice man at social services did not judge me.

I am grateful for my sister, who talked me into getting help.

I am grateful for all this, but especially...

for butter."

Habit #1

"I opened two gifts this morning. They were my eyes."

—ZIG ZIGLAR

THE HABIT OF GRATEFUL #1—DAILY GRATITUDE

• Upon waking, ask yourself, *What am I grateful for today?*

• List three things you are grateful for.

• You can say them out loud, to yourself (internally), or write them down in a journal.

Sight. Smell. Hearing. Touch. Taste. These are your five senses. Let's take a moment to recognize how important each one is. Bill Gates says, "The human body is the most complex system ever created. The more we learn about it, the more appreciation we have about what a rich system it is." The easiest gratitude, right now, is that you are alive. The absolute miracle of your physical body. There are no guarantees you will have a tomorrow.

When I was in the depths of my failing marriage, I was not taking care of my health. My clothes did not fit. I went to the mall with my friend Mary and had to try on bigger sizes. I finally bought a twelve/fourteen and eyed the size six/eight I had been. They looked small. In that moment, I was extra depressed. The reality was I ate junk food and drank each night as soon as I got home to numb the pain. I was not physically active. I had a big stomach roll and loose skin from having three kids. I felt disgusted and every time I saw a picture of myself, I became even more discouraged.

I decided something needed to change. I started going to the local track each morning and walk-running for an hour. I tried the Atkins diet, which helped cut down carbs and junk food. I started making progress and eventually worked up to classes at a local gym.

Each day, I woke up and said to myself, "I am alive. Today is another chance." I made the conscious decision to work on feeling good about my body. Gratitude helped me to stay positive. I made better choices.

Habit #1 is powerful. Start each and every day by telling yourself, "Good morning. I am alive. Today is a gift."

My friend Ben is grateful to be alive. I was recently at a business dinner with Ben, a very successful real estate agent in North Carolina. As we enjoyed our appetizers and cold Sauvignon Blanc, he told me a story from his past.

Before he had kids, he and his wife took a trip to Florida. "I'll never forget when we were getting off the plane, the pilot was female. She was waving to everyone as we deplaned. There were not many female pilots back then, so I was extra impressed," he said. After a few days of vacationing, they decided to visit some family elsewhere and changed their return flight.

In a twist of fate, the flight Ben was originally booked on, ValuJet Flight 592, crashed into the Everglades, killing everyone on board, including Captain Candi Kubeck, who Ben had just met on his flight to Florida just days ago. He saw her photo on the cover of *People* magazine a few days later.

"I still have my paper plane ticket to remind me I could have died in that crash," Ben said.

This brush with death gave him new perspective. He said ever since that day, he feels each morning is a gift he does not take for granted. Ben is one of the kindest people I know.

Chris Klug also had a brush with death. He is a three-time Olympic snowboarder and the only organ transplant recipient to win a medal in the Olympic Games.

In 1991, Chris was diagnosed with primary sclerosing cholangitis (PSC), a rare degenerative bile duct condition affecting the liver. The only known cure was a liver transplant. Chris remained on the transplant waitlist for six years, the last three months in a critical state. During this fragile time, Chris vowed if he made it through, he would do everything he could to make a difference for the thousands of individuals who, like him, waited for a second chance at life. Chris finally received his lifesaving liver transplant on July 28, 2000.

"And I'm here today because of the selfless and heroic decision of another. And that's a pretty humbling gift to receive," Chris told me in an interview.

Only eighteen months after his transplant, Chris took home a bronze medal in the 2002 Winter Olympics in Salt Lake City. The following year, he started the Chris Klug Foundation to promote lifesaving organ and tissue donation and improve the quality of life for those touched by organ donation. Learn more at Chrisklugfoundation.org.

Chris starts every day with the habit of grateful. He shares, "I think gratitude comes easy after getting a second chance at life and standing on death's doorstep. I know it sounds really cliché, but my whole transplant journey from being on a waitlist for six years and receiving a second chance at life really puts things into perspective."

Chris is quick to point out that even in business and family, life is not always perfect. There are still many challenges. He says, "Do we need reminders from time to time? You bet. I try to start each day with a few simple gratitudes. For example, Monday and Tuesday, I woke up at our cabin and said my gratitude, *Thanks for this spectacular property and the opportunity to enjoy it with my family and be totally present and tuned in with no distractions.* So I think gratitudes change daily and weekly, but there is always a silver lining to appreciate."

What I love about Chris Klug is he never gave up on his dream to compete. Anyone would have understood if he called it quits or sat on his couch, but he did not let an illness take him off the mountain. He is grateful every day for the gift of life.

Are you?

GRATITUDE MANTRA FOR HEALTH

Say this out loud to yourself or write it down in a gratitude journal:

My body is a wonder. It breathes, it regenerates, it is the vehicle for my mind and thoughts. I am grateful for my health. Every single day I wake up and I am alive, I am thankful I am here to live another day. Today is a gift.

GRATEFUL FOR FAMILY AND FRIENDS

In her book *A Return to Love*, Marianne Williamson writes, "Something amazing happens when we surrender and just love. We melt into another world, a realm of power already within us. The world changes when we change. The world softens when we soften. The world loves us when we chose to love the world" (Williamson 1996).

Who has made a difference in your life? If you could thank key people right now for all they have done for you or given to you, who would you choose?

Most days, as I am practicing morning gratitude, I think of my children. They bring me such joy. When I consciously express appreciation for each one of them, I picture them in my mind and recount how they make me feel. Although you can be grateful for any three things, try to especially think of people.

By adding this into your morning habit of grateful, you start your day thinking of someone who likes/loves you, and someone who has touched you in some way. Relationships with others make us feel important and valued.

Melissa Wandall found gratitude in a way she never expected. Her husband Mark, was killed in a tragic car crash eighteen years ago. His last words to her as he walked out the door were, "1 love you and I'm going to miss you."

Melissa answered back, "Go get something to eat. We've got the rest of our lives to spend together."

Three hours later she received a horrible call. Mark and her brother were in a car crash one mile from home.

Her entire world changed. She was nine months pregnant.

Melissa recalled, "I was able to say goodbye to my husband, although he'd already passed. So, I thanked him at the scene of the crash for his love and told him I would not let it die. I pledged to grow our love. And I would nurture it even though he was not physically with me. With gratitude."

"Two weeks later, our daughter Madisyn was born. I held her in my arms and I promised her she would know everything about her dad and we would give back through our grief. That we would not be stuck in it. I would not be a broken mommy and she would not be marked by tragedy."

Since then, Melissa has dedicated her life to helping others. She created the Mark Wandall Foundation, a 501 (c)(3) dedicated to facilitating support for children, teens and young adults in grief who have had a parent, sibling or guardian die. Learn more at Themarkwandallfoundation.org.

Melissa says, "Gratitude is born out of love. And when we share our gratitude and love many great things happen. Beautiful people come around to help us on our journey."

Melissa could have easily chosen to live in a victim mindset. No one would have blamed her if she curled up into a ball or checked out. She could have chosen to medicate or numb her pain. Instead, she chose to repurpose her pain and grief and channel it into helping others. Melissa has a superpower of gratitude. She is my hero.

GRATEFUL FOR BASIC NEEDS

"When you are grateful, fear disappears and abundance appears."
—TONY ROBBINS

Remember to appreciate basic needs like shelter, heat/air conditioning, running water, and food. Every single day I look around and I am thankful for all I have. I take a moment to appreciate the fact that I'm very blessed to live in a house; not everyone is so blessed. Think of the homeless, their possessions in a sack or grocery cart. Not everyone has luxuries like running water or hot water.

We need to wake up and appreciate the simple things. Maybe you're just thankful for something simple like heat or air conditioning. Sometimes, when I wake up, I am grateful for a cup of hot coffee. So again, this does not have to be complicated. Just take a moment to appreciate the very basics.

The more I achieve, the more I look around with awe. I never want to take these basic things (shelter, food, water) for granted. Whether it's a new pair of sheets or a pillow or the sound of music in my kitchen, or the way sunlight flows through my house, I always want to appreciate these simple things and not take them for granted.

What if you woke up tomorrow and the only things you had were things you were grateful for? What would that look like?

TIP:

Here are three easy daily gratitudes if you need a prompt:

- I am grateful to be alive.
- I am grateful for family and friends.
- I am grateful for basic needs like food and shelter.

Stronger

I came to the realization the only way I would move up would be to move out. I needed to sell our home. It was the end of another dream. I wanted desperately to keep it and finish the renovations, but it proved too much to heat and maintain.

After countless mediation meetings and then court, we had our final divorce hearing. There were some tearful exchanges and then some anger. I did my best to stay positive. Thankfully, I had family and friends to lean on. One summer day I found myself on the steps of the local courthouse. After I walked through metal detectors and met with our attorney, we signed paperwork and went before the judge. The thump of the gavel. It was official. We were divorced.

My parents had continued to loan me money, and the amount I owed them was staggering. My dad and I had a talk. It became clear to me I needed to sell the house. I had some equity and could pay off debt (including my parents) and use the proceeds to get on my feet.

It was bittersweet, but it was the only way forward.

The kids and I started cleaning out the house. We decided to have a tag sale. I handed each one price tags and markers and urged them to sell things they no longer wanted. They would keep the money from anything they decided to sell. Soon, they had piles of books, old toys, and stuffed animals and were excited to pitch in.

Jolly, our yellow Lab, bounced around and barked at the commotion as crowds of people perused tables set up in the driveway. We had carted down all kinds of things from the attic. Old milk jugs, furniture I never refurbished, and some of the bigger pieces I knew we could not take. It was sad and cathartic all at once.

We made about eight hundred dollars and the kids enjoyed ringing people up and adding up the money they made. Thankfully, my parents helped too. They were a constant pillar of support. It is easy to take family for granted, and prior to my divorce, I did. But during this rough patch, my father constantly came over to fix things. My mother watched the kids so I could work and occasionally stayed overnight. Having their support made me stronger.

I am grateful for my mother and my father. Not only for giving me life, but for teaching me the meaning of life. Family. Love. Helping others. All gifts.

There is growing research about gratitude and how, especially in bad times, it can help us cope. Ryan Fehr, a world-renowned expert on gratitude, states, "During a difficult time, gratitude is more important than ever." He says, "Research shows that gratitude can help us cope with traumatic events, regulate our negative emotions, and improve our well-being" (Kromer 2020).

After the tag sale, I sold my home "off market" to friends look-ing for a project. We set the closing date for the week before Thanksgiving. I threw out *everything.* I purged. I decided to get rid of my wedding dress and unfurled it into the dumpster. Later, we saw cars pull up to the dumpster and pick through trash. The dress stayed at the bottom, yellowing.

I made yet another hard decision. In looking for a rental, I could only have one dog. Not only that, but physically and mentally caring for two dogs plus the kids was too much for me. I felt guilty I did not have more time for two dogs. It was a heart-wrenching decision, but I asked my ex-husband if he would take our Lab, Jolly.

Thankfully, he agreed. He had since moved in with his girl-friend, and they would give her a good home. I knew this was the best decision possible, but it still stung like hell; our family breaking into more pieces. On my final day with her, I gathered her things and took a deep breath. I knelt and gave her a hug, her yellow fur soft against my cheek.

She looked at me with an excited stare (like most Labs do).

"Goodbye, girl. I know you will be happy with your dad. And you'll still have the kids when they visit. Take care of them," I said, convincing myself this was for the best. She panted and nudged me back, hoping for a treat.

"I love you, girl," I said. "And I am sorry. We will miss you. But we will be leaving this place too."

My heart—or what was left of it—ached.

In these moments of depression, I tried to focus on the positive. I was making progress. Baby steps. I had to believe our world would improve. To have faith. The kids deserved better than to live in a half-completed house. The construction, the siding ripped off—it represented my failure. The time had come to build something new.

Though my ex no longer lived with us, his tools were in the garage, and sometimes he pulled into the driveway to grab something. The dogs barked and one of the kids ran out to see him, remembering when he used to come home to them every night like a normal family. Jacob or Amelia clung to their father and begged him to come inside. He explained he was just getting some tools and he needed to go back to his house. He would see them soon. After he left, there were tears. The pain was still raw.

It would be better to find our own place; a new home with new beginnings. I had to be strong, so I was.

When I was little, my dad would take me fishing. We caught trout and he tied them up with a metal safety pin type thing through their gills. When we had a bunch, he took them home. Then he showed me how to gut each of them: shiny bellies slit open, then the insides ripped out until all that remained was a nice clean hull. He pan-fried them and we ate the delicate meat. The skin got a nice crisp.

My best analogy for divorce was the fish gutting process. I was never quite the same. My insides were gone.

And yet the gutting made room for a transformation.

If a dead trout could turn into a butterfly, then that would be what happened next.

KEEP DIGGING

"Whether you think you can or you can't you're right."

—HENRY FORD

There is a motivational theory called Maslow's Hierarchy of Needs. It states we must first satisfy our most basic needs before we can feel totally secure and move toward self-actualization. If we are so busy focusing on hunger, shelter, and basic stability, then it is harder to have the attention needed to chase your dreams professionally and personally (Maslow 1943).

Once those basic needs are met (food, shelter, and security), as well as areas like friendship and relationships, more growth occurs. Belongingness refers to a human emotional need for inter-personal relationships, affiliating, connectedness, and being part of a group. Like friendship, intimacy, trust, acceptance, and love.

Each day I worked on myself. I refused to be a victim.

I made a list:

- Sell house and pay off debt.
- Finish college degree.
- Get healthy and lose weight.
- Be the best mom possible.
- Find love again.

Not only did I focus on gratitude in every situation, but I worked on programming myself with the right mindset. I got my head back into the game and started to rebuild my real estate career. In the words of my dear friend Mary, I reminded myself: You are strong. You are kind. You are smart. And you are beautiful, inside and out. Even though I did not always believe those words, I kept repeating them.

Positive affirmations can help you change the way you think. You can reprogram your mind with words. There is evidence-based research demonstrating that affirmations, like prayer, can activate certain neural pathways in the brain and lead to the desired outcome (Cascio 2015).

You've probably affirmed yourself without even realizing it by telling yourself things like:

"I can do this."

"I've got what it takes."

"I know I can win."

Jim Miller is a successful real estate coach and a good friend. He, too, survived the real estate crash of 2008–09, and in a recent interview, we talked about how that shaped both of us; each in our own way.

Jim says, "Like many in our industry, I struggled mightily between 2007 and 2012. I went on a self-development journey to identify those areas of my life and business that needed a major overhaul while struggling with the fact that my current situation was less than ideal."

Jim had to reinvent himself. He studied, read, and emerged stronger and better for surviving the market meltdown. Now he inspires countless others.

Jim created this brilliant affirmation:

I am so happy and grateful that money, success, and introductions flow to me in ever increasing quantities from a myriad of different sources and for the betterment of all those involved. My life is perfect. Every day, in every way, I'm getting better and better.

Even now I say affirmations out loud and write them on paper. This has been crucial to improving my mindset. When you add affirmations to gratitude, you have a supercharged power current. It works.

In May 2022, *Vogue* published an article called, "A Deep Dive into the Science behind Self-Affirmations" (Mjaaset 2022). The author, Nina Mjaaset, suggests choosing from the following affirmations:

- I surround myself with people who want the best for me

- I am in control of my life

- I deserve happiness, health, and love

- I love my body and all it does for me

- Loving myself comes easily to me

- I am open to receive love

- I am at peace with where I am

- I am constantly growing and evolving into the best version of myself

- I am proud of who I am today

- My relationships are becoming deeper, stronger, and more stable each day

- I am blessed with a wonderful family and loyal friends

- I radiate charm, beauty, and kindness

- I am worthy of a healthy relationship filled with love

- The more I love those around me, the more love I receive in return

- I am attracting genuine connection

- I am loved more than I ever thought possible

Take your pick. Any of these affirmations can be transformative. Circle the ones that resonate most with you.

AFFIRMATION "HOW TO"

Spend some time thinking about what you really want to accomplish. Are you stuck? Is there something you would love to make happen or work on?

Perhaps it is losing weight, or a new job, or being more organized. Think about what you want to make happen and write it down. It's best to focus on one goal at a time. You can make your goal broad or specific.

SAY YOUR AFFIRMATIONS OUT LOUD.

The perfect time to remember to do this is when you first wake up in the morning, when you are getting ready for the day, in the shower, while doing your hair, or getting dressed.

USE THE PRESENT TENSE.

Tell yourself this thing you want is already happening. For example, you might say, "I am an excellent golfer" rather than "I can become an excellent golfer." This focuses your attention on shifting your beliefs rather than setting a goal.

DON'T BE NEGATIVE.

The goal is to shift into a positive mindset. Make sure your affirmation does not have any negativity. For example, instead of saying, "I will no longer make poor choices in food," you might say, "I enjoy making healthy choices."

IMPACT.

Be sure to use affirmations for the changes you want to see happen in your life. Focus on yourself and what you can control. Repeat your affirmation daily for at least thirty days. Others report success by writing out their affirmation over and over about twenty-five times on a piece of paper in addition to saying them out loud.

Jim Carrey, the famous actor, said: "I begin all my days with twenty minutes of visualization. This moment is when I have my first chance to change things. If you do it in the morning, it can change your whole day" (Digital 2021). In an interview with Oprah Winfrey, he described how he visualized himself someday being a famous actor and even wrote himself a check for ten million dollars with the date October 1995 on it. Five years later, in the fall of 1995, he was offered ten million dollars for *Dumb and Dumber*.

Jim also pointed out to Oprah, "But then I worked for it. I didn't just go make a sandwich" (Epic 2020).

If you are willing to do the work and stay positive, good things will happen. Not only did I use affirmations and gratitude, but I committed to starting each day in a positive mindset. It turns out that not only can a morning routine change your day but it can also change your life.

GOODBYE DUTTON ROAD

On closing day, I went to our little house for the final walk-through. As I entered, I was shocked at how different it looked empty. It was a warm day for fall, and the windows were cracked open. The curtains rustled in the breeze like a dream sequence. Surreal.

I never thought my life would make this hook-like turn and lead to divorce and leaving our house. As I walked into the living room, staring at the fireplace we built, I remembered little Amelia, age one, in her red Christmas dress sitting on the couch beside me. How I cradled Jacob in my arms and rocked him. He toddled after his big brother endlessly in this house, cruising over these uneven wood floors. And our first big snowstorm, how Triston (in full snow pants) and Jolly ran circles in the backyard. The memories circled like leaves swirling in the wind.

Goodbye, house.

The sun shined through the windows. I stood in a big yellow ray of it, letting it warm me.

I caught a glimpse of my shadow. I stood taller. The new me. I could just make out the edges of her. I started to like this new me. She was stronger. Smarter. I wrapped my arms across my chest and hugged myself.

This guilt jacket was coming off. It had to go. I hung it on a peg in the hallway. I was ready.

Next chapter.

Morning Routine

"You think this is just another day in your life? It's not just another day. It's the one day that is given to you today. It's given to you. It's a gift. It's the only gift that you have right now, and the only appropriate response is gratefulness."

—LOUIE SCHWARTZBERG

Before I started a daily habit of grateful, I hated mornings.

I hated the sound of the alarm and felt such sadness and despair. I did not want to get out of bed and would lay with the blankets snug against my face, clinging to every last second. I knew all the hard things I had to face when my feet hit the ground.

Mornings sucked.

My transition to a morning routine did not happen overnight. It was the culmination of many things. But when it happened, it was as if someone finally turned a light on. Imagine a broken lamp sitting on the floor. It is not plugged in. The shade is dingy and crooked. It needs a new bulb. That was me.

First, I had to get the lamp off the floor. I had to look at it and say, "This is a great lamp. I am going to use it." So, I went out and bought a new bulb. But the lamp needed a power source. I had to find a spot with electricity.

Gratitude was the switch. I was the lamp.

It turns out, I am not alone. Bob Burg is coauthor of *The Go-Giver*. He shared how focusing on a habit of gratitude changed his entire mindset. He made the decision to proactively be grateful for a period of time. In an interview, Bob told me, "I put up yellow sticky notes all over the house—on the bathroom mirror, on my computer, in my car, everywhere. And I just wrote in a big circle, gratitude. So I would see it all the time. And I would just focus on that."

He noticed an immediate difference.

"Very quickly, like within week, I just changed. I mean, it just made such a huge difference in my life. But here's the thing, remember it feels good to feel grateful. Right? So you want more of it. I love to practice gratitude. It's a lot easier than staying on a diet. Because it feels good to be grateful. It's easy." To this day, Bob consciously focuses on what (and who) he is grateful for.

Atomic Habits author, James Clear, is an expert at routine and habits. James created a morning routine to maximize his mindset. After waking up with no alarm (unless he needs to catch a flight or has an appointment), Clear takes a shower, drinks a glass of water, and then "writes three things I'm grateful for, reads twenty pages of a book, then gets into whatever work is for the day," Clear told *My Morning Routine* (Xander 2014). He says, "Twenty-five thousand times you get to open your eyes, face the day, and decide what to do next. I don't know about you, but I've let a lot of those mornings slip by."

It seems many high-performance individuals not only have a morning routine but also use the habit of gratitude as a means of shifting into a positive mindset. In the study "Counting Blessings Versus Burdens" (Emmons 2003), researchers documented how a grateful outlook of participants impacted one's psychological and physical well-being. In studies one and two, participants kept weekly or daily records of their moods, coping behaviors, health behaviors, physical symptoms, and overall life appraisals. The gratitude outlook groups exhibited heightened well-being across several, though not all, of the outcome measures across three controlled studies, relative to the comparison groups (Emmons 2003).

Results suggest a conscious focus on blessings may have emotional and interpersonal benefits. There are numerous other studies concluding the same.

Now I love mornings. They are exciting. Each day brings with it such promise. A new chance. Endless opportunity.

As Zig Ziglar said, "I opened two gifts this morning. They were my eyes." This stays with me. Especially during times when I have lost a friend or family member. It reaffirms the fact that life is a gift. As James Clear reminds us, we only get twenty-five thousand mornings. Shouldn't we appreciate each one?

If you ever have trouble thinking of three things to be grateful for in the morning, be grateful you are alive. Start with that.

WHY IT WORKS

Dr. Seligman states that the first thing we must know about happiness is there is an element called positive affectivity. These are people cheerful and merry by natural disposition, but roughly 50 percent of the world is not positively affective. These are people who have to learn to be positive, learn optimism, and learn there's hope in the future. The good news is it is teachable (Seligman 2022).

When we talk about the benefits of gratitude, daily commitment is crucial. Emmons and Michael McCullough state gratitude can be generally distilled to a two-step cognitive process: 1) "Recognizing that one has obtained a positive outcome" and 2) "Recognizing that there is an external source for this positive outcome" (Emmons & McCullough 2003). By implementing the morning routine, you tap into this two-step cognitive process. It is the perfect way to begin your day. Starting each day with gratitude first thing ensures you won't forget.

Dr. Kim Knox says, "The thoughts we have like, *I'm never going to do this. I don't deserve this,* are super easy to fall into. They come naturally to people. But we can't start thinking positively or put that energy into gratitude unless we train our brains to do that."

It's like running a marathon. My husband is like, this marathon needs you and I'm like, I hate running. I don't want to run twenty miles. But you can't get out and just run twenty miles, right? It takes a lot of practice. Gratitude is a positive mind frame practice. People don't just jump out of bed and say all of a sudden I'm going to be a gratitude warrior. It takes time and practice and energy to tame those negative thoughts.

Gratitude is a very powerful thing. The single strength that correlates most with happiness is gratitude. Grateful people are inclined to be happier; they have a bounce to their step.

The one thing all humans have in common is each of us wants to be happy, says David Steindl-Rast, a monk and interfaith scholar. And happiness, he suggests, is born from gratitude. In his TED talk, "Want to Be Happy? Be Grateful," he elaborates:

> How is the connection between happiness and gratefulness? Many people would say well, that's very easy. When you are happy, you're grateful. But think again. Is it really the happy people that are grateful? We all know quite a number of people who have everything that it would take to be happy and they are not happy because they want something else or they want more of the same. And we all know people who have lots of misfortune, misfortune that we ourselves would not want to have, and they are deeply happy. They radiate happiness. You are surprised. Why? Because they are grateful. (Steindl-Rast 2013)

This explains how, even in my darkest times, gratitude for simple things helped me. Even when I did not want to get out of bed, I focused on my children and how grateful I was to be a parent. To be loved. I thought about the small wins, like clean sheets, my health, or not being homeless. Even when I was poor, I felt rich in some ways. And that matters.

Dr. Seligman shares:

A lot of people don't have gratitude; I've had to learn it. I remember on my sixtieth birthday, I brought a lot of people together from my past and my present. And I realized for the first time that my life was not an autobiography, but it was a biography in which all these people had made me what I became. I think it's very important for people like me, people who are not naturally cheery and merry to learn gratitude and to exercise gratitude. (Seligman 2016)

Here Seligman references his gratitude for the people who made his life rich. Appreciating your relationships is key in feeling loved. In fact, gratitude can make you feel connected and not lonely by simply appreciating the people in your life.

Gratitude can be learned. There are many words for it: an exercise, a habit, or even a gratitude intervention.

MORNING GRATITUDE

"When you arise in the morning, think of what a precious privilege it is to be alive—to breathe, to think, to enjoy, to love."

—MARCUS AURELIUS

Upon waking each day, focus on gratitude. As soon as your alarm goes off and your eyes open, think about how grateful you are that you have the gift of a new day. You are alive. By refocusing yourself each day with gratitude, you supercharge your intention and will be amazed at all the wonderful miracles that can happen.

Try a daily mantra. Keep it simple. Say this to yourself:

I am grateful to be alive.

Today is a gift.

I am grateful for _____.

As you open your eyes and wake up, resist the urge to pick up your phone and check email or social media right away. Instead, spend some time focused on gratitude. Now, think of everything you are grateful for.

Here are some of mine: a house, the sun rising, coffee, my health, my kids, my dog, the sunshine, a good book, my hearing, my friends, and running hot water.

Gratitude is very easy to find once you look for it. This is the easiest way to begin focusing on gratitude as a habit. Associate waking up with asking yourself what you are grateful for. It should only take a few minutes. Over time it should become second nature.

Make a promise to yourself that you will begin each day with gratitude.

Cold Heart

Winter in New England was a series of blizzards and freezing mush. So was my heart. The divorce and subsequent attempts at finding love left me feeling bleak.

Would I ever find love again? My heart was a tundra.

The kids and I moved into a rental house with electric heat, a funky kitchen, and spiral staircase. "Mom, it's so warm in here," Triston said and I smiled because for the first winter: no draft. With the house sale proceeds, I finally had a financial cushion. I paid my debts and did not have to renew government assistance. No more food stamps.

Thankfully, our new home had a bright red wood stove that helped with heating. The responsibility of getting wood from outside and constantly keeping the fire blazing offered a comforting routine. I loved a fire. It heated the house to a warm and cozy seventy-five degrees. It was slowly thawing out the cold parts of me. Could my heart ever love again? I was not sure.

One night I carried a bucket of hot ashes outside. As I carefully made my way to the snow-covered stairs, the railing gave way and I tumbled hard into the snow, screaming as hot embers landed on top of me. I laid there in the snow for a moment, spitting out god knows what and shaking off ashes. I sat up. I rubbed soot from my eyes. I had a moment where I felt bad for myself and almost started to cry.

But then I started thinking about what I looked like. Flowery pajamas under my big puffy (and now scorched) winter jacket, a face of soot, messy bun hair, and two big circles around my eyes (thank goodness I had on my glasses). I started to laugh.

I was alone. And it was okay.

Because I was tough.

I could do this.

The kids and I settled into a new routine. We had created a new normal for the four of us. Triston was starting high school and growing fast. A faint mustache. Jacob was thriving in middle school, and Amelia in elementary school. It was like the training wheels came off, and suddenly the single mom thing was working.

I was still careful with my budget but could afford groceries and the occasional meal out. I felt gratitude each time I went to the grocery store knowing my card would not be declined, and if the kids wanted ice cream, we could go.

I was more balanced at work, and post-divorce I was more focused. I enrolled in online classes once again and chipped away at finishing my college degree. Selling real estate paid the bills, but I longed for a different path. I even thought about law school, though it seemed like a reach. I liked the legal side of work, and being an attorney was something I often considered. I also wanted to help other women and moms.

To reference Maslow, I attained my basic needs and jumped up the pyramid toward my higher self. Maslow wrote:

> It is quite true that man lives by bread alone—when there is no bread. But what happens to man's desires when there is plenty of bread [...]? At once other (and "higher") needs emerge and these, rather than physiological hungers, dominate the organism. And when these in turn are satisfied, again new (and still "higher") needs emerge and so on. (Maslow 1943)

Every morning started with gratitude. I woke up and felt the warmth of the house. I put on a robe and lit the woodstove and felt grateful. Each night I tucked in the kids, turned off the lights, and told myself, "You can do this."

I noticed other moms picked up on my positive mindset. Women in our community reached out to ask divorce questions. It brought a sense of relief to share my stories, and I encouraged other single moms to stay positive. Around this time, I read *Eat, Pray, Love* by Elizabeth Gilbert. It was like a bible for divorced women. Even though I couldn't afford to eat and cry my way through Italy, so many of her personal stories and reflections about love lost resonated with me. I always had a few secondhand copies and handed them out.

Gilbert writes, "In the end, though, maybe we must all give up trying to pay back the people in this world who sustain our lives. In the end, maybe it's wiser to surrender before the miraculous scope of human generosity and to just keep saying thank you, forever and sincerely, for as long as we have voices" (Gilbert 2007).

With each burning fire, I knew that soon spring would emerge. The snow would melt.

I had some new rules for myself:

- No drinking alcohol at home
- Focus on self-care and a healthy lifestyle
- Less TV, more books
- Daily affirmations and gratitude
- Get comfortable with being alone

In time, I started feeling ready for a relationship. I visualized someone tall, with kind blue eyes. Someone who would wrap me in big arms and keep me safe. Someone I could laugh with, talk to, and someone who would support my dreams.

I spent a lot of time thinking about the type of person I wanted to find. I believe we attract what we want in life, but first we need to have intention. You have to know what you want. In detail.

I made a list:

- Tall and attractive
- Financially responsible
- Educated
- Kind
- Fun but not wild
- Secure

- Intelligent
- Good with kids

Modern dating was weird, and Match.com was the new norm. I found myself disappointed and could not seem to find the right person. I had a few casual relationships. Nothing stuck.

My childhood friend, Jamie, called one weekend. She was in town. "We need to take you out for a proper girls' night out!"

"I really don't feel like going out." It was cold. And I was tired.

"It will be good for you to have some fun."

"What is fun?" I joked.

"Come on!"

"Okay."

We met in Litchfield and carpooled to a bar in a neighboring city.

"Oh my gosh, you look amazing!" she said.

I had finally shed my depression weight and was down from an all-time high of a size fourteen to a size six. I committed to being physically active and eating healthy. "Thank you," I said and hugged her. I had on a pair of dark jeans and a formfitting black top.

We paid the cover charge and were given hand stamps. The Red Door was a younger but mixed crowd. Music blasted and we could barely hear each other. Brick walls were the backdrop to a long bar packed with couples and singles as the bartender shook a cocktail over his head loudly and another poured draft beers. Further inside, a rock band was on stage and a decent sized crowd was watching, some dancing. We got some drinks and hung out on the periphery of the dance floor. The last thing I expected to find was anyone worth dating; it was all about having some fun or "getting out there" as my friends kept saying.

Out of the corner of my eye, I saw a gorgeous tall guy dancing with a beer in his hand. He was singing, twirling a girl around with a group of friends. He had dirty blond hair and a green sweater with two large stripes running down the arms.

My heart thumped and I took a closer look. He looked familiar. That face. Hair gelled back. I got closer and locked eyes with him.

I *froze.*

It was the social worker from the day I applied for food stamps. And we were staring at each other. In a bar. I suddenly felt so embarrassed and exposed.

"Oh my god," I said to my friend Jamie.

"Are you okay?" she asked, looking at the guy I was staring at. "Stripes?"

I nodded.

"Okay, he's hot, but you need to chill."

"I think I know him."

He turned and looked at me again and smiled. Wait. Could it be him? I wondered. Perhaps it was wishful thinking. What were the odds?

I took a gulp of liquid courage and walked over to him. "Nice stripes," I smiled and walked away. Yep. It was him. Oh. My. God.

"Hey. Where are you going?" he called after me.

I could not believe it. A wave of excitement ran over me to have found him again. Everything had changed. I was not on food stamps. I had sold my house.

I walked to the bar and sat down. He appeared next to me.

"You look familiar."

"We have met."

"I thought so."

"Thank you for all you did to help me."

"I am glad it worked out."

"I sold my house. That saved me. I am in a good place now."

"I'm glad. You look amazing," he said appreciatively. "Divorced?"

"Finalized."

"Congratulations. I think?"

I nodded. "Yes."

"You have kids, right?"

I gulped. This was the moment most guys would wince, make an excuse, and walk away. "Yep. Three. And two dogs. Well, actually one dog."

He stared into my eyes, searching. It was an electric jolt.

"You can run now," I said, half-kidding.

He moved closer. "I am not going anywhere."

I am not sure if it was the alcohol or the way he looked at me, but I leaned in and gave him a kiss on the lips. The rest of the world melted away.

"Can I call you?" he asked.

"I would love that." I gave him my phone number and said good night.

The next stay, I was giddy. I stared at my phone and willed him to text or call. He needed to make the first move. Plus, I did not have his number. Weeks went by.

"I am sure he will call," my sister said. "Think positive."

I worried I had too much baggage.

Another week went by. Of course I had baggage, who was I kidding. Perhaps he wasn't attracted to me. I was a mom of three.

If you have ever seen the movie *Jerry Maguire*, there is a scene where the sports agent, Jerry, confides to Rod (his friend/star football player) that dating Dorothy (who happens to be a single mom) is complicated:

Rod: "I feel for you, man. But a real man wouldn't shoplift the pootie from a single mom."

Jerry: "I didn't shoplift the pootie."

[Rod gives Jerry a long, knowing look.]

Jerry: "All right. I shoplifted the pootie" (Crowe 1996).

Dating a single mom is not like dating someone without kids. I wondered if I was too complicated. My heart tugged. I went on a few dates and kept busy. Between work and carting the kids around to sports and helping them with homework and friends, the days/nights went by in a whirlwind.

One night after school I told the kids, "Put on your nicest clothes."

"Why?" they asked. "Where are we going?"

"The orphanage?" Triston asked.

"What? Why would you ever say that?"

"You said to put on nice clothes. I think that's what they say in the movies before you go to the orphanage."

Amelia looked at me in horror. She and Jacob had just been in the musical *Annie*.

"I would *never* take you to an orphanage! I'm trying to take you out to a fancy dinner!" I did not know if I should laugh or cry.

"Just kidding," he said.

I took them to a nice restaurant on the Green. "Order whatever you want," I said as we slid into a booth. I was so grateful, knowing we could afford the luxury of eating out.

"Thanks Mom."

"Thanks."

"Thanks."

Each little voice was a heart-melt. My babies.

On the way home, Triston sat in front with me and blasted the music as we all sang (screamed really) to "Bohemian Rhapsody." I laughed so hard I almost peed my pants. Life was good.

We got home and I let out our dog, Frankie. It was March. The snow had melted. Soon, spring would be here.

My phone rang and I let it go to voicemail.

Later, I listened to the message. It was Stripes. His name was Ian.

It's about time, I said to myself.

It had taken him over a month to finally call and ask me out. I was mad he took so long, but agreed to go out on a date. We met for drinks at a local pub. When I saw him, my heart did backflips. He was tall, kind, and educated. Well-spoken. Fun but not wild. He was everything on my list and more.

After we sat, talking for an hour, it was time to go. Ian walked me to my car. Then he pulled me into his arms. My cheek fit perfectly against his big, wide chest. His heavy arms wrapped around me. It was like nothing I had ever felt.

A few months later Ian and I moved in together.

Then soon after, we married and had a son, Liam.

Our family was complete.

A NEW START

It was closing day, and we had already done the walk-through of our new house. Ian and I were officially homeowners. Liam was now two, and toddling around the tile and wood floors. I couldn't believe how beautiful our new house was, with a huge kitchen and granite counters, formal dining and living room, and a den with a gas fireplace. Crown molding. The upstairs had a bedroom suite with walk-in closet, office, and an over-sized soaking tub in the large bathroom. Double sinks. It was a short walk to the private lake with tennis courts, clubhouse, and beach; the same private beach my friend Mary once took us to.

The kids ran around, excited. "Why do you guys get the biggest room?" Jacob asked.

"Wow. It just keeps going," Triston said. Our bedroom is huge. I pinched myself.

"Mom!" Amelia yelled. "Mom, I want the other room. The red one."

"Can I put my guitar in the basement?" Triston asked.

"Knock your socks off."

Liam clapped and wrapped himself around Ian's leg. "Daddy. Mommy."

Ian picked up Liam and came up beside me. He hugged me. "I love you," he said. "And I love our new house. We are very lucky."

In those moments, my heart burst with joy. Not just because we bought a house together and finally have our own home, but because he was by my side.

I am grateful for our new home.

I am grateful the kids are happy and healthy.

I am grateful I have a husband who encourages me.

I am grateful we have food in our kitchen.

And butter.

Habit #2—Be the Sunshine

- Look for opportunities to appreciate others throughout your day.

- Tell everyone you meet in person that you "appreciate them" when you can.

- Use the words "I appreciate you" in every conversation possible.

- Perform acts of kindness to inspire others.

Gratitude is the act of expressing appreciation for what you have (as opposed to what you do not have). It is an exercise in acknowledging the goodness in your life. Open your eyes to everyone in your orbit and look for ways to tell others you *appreciate them.*

It's simple! Everyone can do it—kids and adults. Regardless of your job title or where you live, when you choose to tell others you appreciate them, you integrate gratitude as a habit into your life.

Let's explore.

Imagine this: It's a Monday. You overslept and when you look at the time, you realize you are late for work. The stress of the impending day makes you agitated and cranky. Your significant other is in a bad mood. You missed trash day and your car is running on empty. You feel your blood pressure rising and are spiraling. You want to lash out at everyone or crawl into a hole and just give up. Sound familiar?

Instead, let's consider this: As you awaken, you think about three things you are grateful for. You start with: *I am alive. Today is a gift.* You then list other things you are grateful for like: *a home, water, food, family, pets.* When you see your significant other, you hug them and tell them, "Good morning. I appreciate you." They smile and rub your back. When you walk your dog and see the mailman, you say, "Good morning! Thanks for my mail. I appreciate you." The mailman thanks you and smiles back. You might decide to pause for a moment and enjoy the beauty of flowers or to pet your furry friend. You are like sunshine, radiating positivity to all those around you. It's infectious.

Let's remember that gratitude has physical effects on the body. Just like when you go to the gym and work biceps, the neurons in your brain are activated every time you practice gratitude. They get stronger.

In an article for *HuffPost*, Emily Fletcher, the founder of Ziva (a meditation site), calls gratitude a natural antidepressant. She writes:

Production of dopamine and serotonin increases, and these neurotransmitters then travel neural pathways to the "bliss" center of the brain—similar to the mechanisms of many antidepressants. Practicing gratitude, therefore, can be a way to naturally create the same effects of medications and create feelings of contentment. (Fletcher 2017)

As you consciously frame your day with gratitude and look to appreciate those around you, you will notice a gentleness in your soul. You will feel better. Your mindset will shift into the positive. Little things that used to upset you will seem trivial. You learn how to live in a more relaxed and balanced state.

Habit number two shifts your focus. Instead of only thinking about yourself, you actively focus on others. There is a world around you. Connect with that world and the people you meet.

Thich Nhat Hanh (1926–2022) was a Vietnamese Buddhist Zen Master, poet, peace activist, and one of the most revered spiritual teachers in the world.

In his book *The Art of Living*, he writes:

> Throughout our life we produce energy. We say things and do things, and every thought, every word, and every act carries our signature. What we produce as thoughts, as speech, as action, continues to influence the world, and that is our continuation body. Our actions carry us into the future. We are like stars whose light energy continues to radiate across the cosmos millions of years after they become extinct. [...] Use your time wisely. Every moment it is possible to think, say, or do something that inspires hope, forgiveness, and

compassion. You can do something to protect and help others and our world. We have to train ourselves in the art of right thinking so we can produce positive, nourishing thoughts every day. (Hanh 2017)

Let gratitude be our light; the sunshine to everyone we meet.

CONVERSATIONS WITH GRATITUDE

Think about the conversations you have with others. How do they begin and end? Are they right to the point? Do you take time to even acknowledge the other person? Do you jump into the purpose of the conversation like a bulldozer? That used to be me. I was so focused on the outcome of a conversation that I wanted to skip right through the talking part. *Seriously.*

When we approach a conversation, we have a need, especially a conversation we initiate. If you have been on the receiving end of someone who showed you no regard and no personal connection, you might have felt "worked over."

Consider the opposite. Have you ever gotten a call from someone that made you feel *so special* you felt energized just talking to them? You ended your conversation and felt happy. Uplifted. Appreciated. Gratitude infused into conversation is a game changer.

Start each conversation by telling the other person you appreciate them.

You can say:

- I want you to know how much I appreciate you.

- I am so thankful we are speaking/connecting.

- I really appreciate your time, thank you.

- I am grateful to have an opportunity to see you/talk with you because...

This works especially well if you need to have a tough conversation. Start with simple gratitude.

Gratitude helps a conversation feel safe. The book *Crucial Conversations: Tools for Talking When Stakes Are High* offers some steps for mastering very difficult conversations. It focuses on how to hold such conversations in a positive space when surrounded by highly charged emotions. Based on twenty-five years of research conducted with over twenty thousand people, the method has seven steps. The first (and I think most important) is "Start with the Heart (i.e., empathy and positive intent). You always approach the other person with empathy—in other words, sharing a gratitude. This sets the tone and works like magic" (Patterson et al. 2021).

PERSONAL RELATIONSHIPS

As the parent of three teenagers, tough conversations and high emotion have been a constant. Each child has unique needs and is wired differently. Many times in the past, I responded negatively or matched their challenging tone with a harsh "let me show you." This never worked.

By readjusting mindset first, the conversation can be more productive or at least not combative. The easiest way to do this is to try to go to a place of gratitude. Take a pause, take a breath, and remind yourself the reasons why you are grateful for that person before you begin talking. This can put things in perspective for your personal emotions.

Next, recognize the value of your relationship by telling them you appreciate them. It's simple. Just say, "I want to let you know I appreciate you." If you can also add in why you appreciate them, that's great, but if you can't, that's fine too.

Then take a big pause.

The next step in the conversation should be identifying your common goal(s) to make it feel safe.

Move on to identifying the problem and work as a team to problem solve.

Always conclude by thanking the other person.

When this is genuine, it works wonders. Empathy and appreciation are always the best way to problem solve.

My friend Mel shared that when her teenage son got on her nerves (like most teenagers do), she changed his profile photo on her phone to him as a chubby-cheeked adorable toddler. She said, "Every time I saw his little boy face pop up on my phone, I reminded myself to be grateful for this boy. Before I answered the phone, I concentrated on the love I have for him.

Using gratitude, I was able to reset my emotions and be open to a tough conversation."

SHARING GRATITUDE

Harvard Medical School states that gratitude is a thankful appreciation for what one receives, tangible or intangible, as they acknowledge the goodness in their lives (Schultz 2018).

I now start my professional meetings asking everyone to share a gratitude. If it's a large group, I ask them to share a gratitude with the person next to them. It raises the energy level in the room. I highly suggest this to infuse positivity into a gathering.

It is impossible to be angry and grateful at the same time. When you find yourself getting angry about something like the missing sesame chicken from your takeout order, or your spouse's muddy boot prints in the kitchen, or when someone cuts you off on the highway, take a moment and think about all the things you are grateful for. It takes a little practice but diffuses anger.

Colleen Barry, the CEO of a large real estate firm (and one of the smartest people I know), tries to use gratitude every day as a leader. She goes out of her way to thank her staff and looks for opportunities to appreciate others.

Recently, Colleen and I sat down and discussed how using gratitude has made us both better leaders. She shared:

The way to change the world is by acknowledging those around you. That's really it. I mean, it ripples outwards.

The ripples can go on for generations if you help somebody understand that they are valued, and the value in helping others. They will pass that on to their progeny. And so, I think that is how to change the world. It's not through giant grand gestures. It's just by being kind, warm, and caring to the people around you. That's it.

And not only does Colleen feel good about her leadership style, but her people adore her. She is revered as one of the greatest CEOs in our industry. Everyone who meets her comes away feeling valued. I love that!

ACKNOWLEDGING OTHERS

"As dusk arrives I look up to the sky and touch the beauty of mother earth. My heart fills with gratitude."
—SISTER TRANG GIAC MINH (HANH 2017)

Keep your antenna up. When someone does something kind for you, tell them how much you appreciate them. Here's the thing: the more you say thank you, the better you will feel. It will feel so good, you will start looking for people to thank.

When I am at a business event, I make a point to greet all the venue staff and say hello. I thank them for their service and let them know how much we appreciate their efforts. You can see how it brightens their day. They smile and you can see their eyes light up. And I genuinely appreciate all they do for us.

A friend of mine, Maria Vitale, told me she makes it a point to chat with everyone in her office building. She has met some extremely wealthy people and they have become clients. She has gotten to know the janitor on her floor and he, too, is a client. She says, "Everyone deserves gratitude and everyone deserves a high level of service, no matter who they are."

As students of gratitude, we have an obligation to be the sunshine to those around us, especially once we have personally experienced the positive benefits from a habit of grateful. Habit number two is crucial because it requires you to consciously look for others throughout your day and appreciate them. It might be the cashier at Walgreens or a coffee barista at Starbucks. Look them in the eyes and say, "Thank you. I really appreciate you."

You may be pleasantly surprised at how they smile back and the feeling of joy you experience. Maybe they will in turn be nicer to the people they see that day. Visualize your gratitude rippling out into the universe.

How many people can you appreciate with your words in one day? In a week?

Be the sunshine.

The Climb

Real estate has been good to me. I got my real estate license about twenty years ago, around the time I became a mom and got tired of working as a videographer and editor. Triston was two years old, and I was driving back and forth to Hartford working the evening shift. I got hired for vacation relief, which meant I was a floater videographer and editor for a CBS affiliate news station.

I grew up watching Denise D'Ascenzo and Al Terzi, as well as Gayle King and Dennis House. My grandmother thought I was famous just because I worked at a television station. I brought her in to visit and she was so starstruck I thought she would pass out.

Denise was one of the kindest people with whom I worked. She always went out of her way to make conversation and had a warmth that radiated to others. Gayle also took note of my inspirational notepad (a gift from Mary) and shared stories from her television career. The night shift has its own vibe, and I enjoyed learning from some of the best in the industry.

I started out in the editing bay, where we monitored feeds from around the world and edited clips or stories. My time there was high energy, fast paced, and at times stressful. I started going out into the field more with an AP Wire pager, three-chip camera, and stack of maps. I drove a Jeep Cherokee that said "News Crew" on the side. This was pre-GPS, if you can imagine. One night, as I left the studio at 11:30 p.m., the news desk asked me to catch some B-roll for a report on a shooting in Frog Hollow. Not really knowing the neighborhood, I drove out there and parked behind flashing red and blue lights just past midnight.

"Go home, white girl," someone shouted. They screamed some other not-so-nice obscenities.

A police officer approached and stood next to me protectively. "Did you get your video footage? You should leave. It's not safe out here."

Two weeks later, I covered a drive-by shooting in front of a crack house. I filmed the bullet holes that came through the window of the house next door. There were no casualties, but the bullets almost hit children inside. By the time I got back to the station, unloaded, and drove home, I was exhausted. My eyes kept closing during my drive.

I wondered what I was doing with my life. Although I loved filming and editing, the news was mostly horrible. Murders. Shootings. Tragedies. It was draining.

Right around that time, my then-husband and I decided to try to buy a house. We outgrew our little apartment and I wanted out. We looked in a nearby affluent town. A family friend sold real estate, and she patiently helped us for a few months. I still don't even know how we got a mortgage. We sold personal items, like jewelry and guitars, and even turned in change jars to patch together a small down payment.

We became the proud owners of a little antique home built in 1875. There were bats in the attic, wallpaper with a pink poodle motif (I am not joking), along with lots of leaded glass windows, a kitchen from 1950, and a damp basement, *but* it was in a quaint town with an amazing school system and had a big yard leading to a river. I was twenty-four and believed we could fix anything.

At that time, I was pregnant with our second child, Jacob. Triston was three, and we just brought home our dog, Jolly.

We had done some water testing on the well. The day after the closing, we got a fax that the well had MTBE and some other chemicals.

"What is MTBE?" I asked. "Is that like a mineral?"

"It's found in gasoline," the water lab technician said. "Methyl tertiary-butyl ether. Best to call the health department. Do not ingest it."

I stared at the water faucet. "Do not ingest it? Our water?" I thought I might faint.

We had scraped together every penny and now we couldn't drink our water. A nightmare.

After a year of talks with our neighbors and the town, we got access to safe drinking water. I had become the unofficial leader and learned how to guide multiple parties to an agreement. One of my neighbors, a well-known real estate broker, said to me, "You should go into real estate. You are a natural."

Our family friend (who owned a small real estate firm) offered to sponsor me, and I looked up the information to sign up for the class. The total cost with books was over a thousand dollars and it was out of reach. I had cut back on my hours at the TV station after having baby number two, but I could at least try to find a solution.

I called the community college and asked if they might work with me on a payment plan. I was shocked when they made the exception.

After months of night classes, I passed my exam. I got my license and worked afternoons and weekends to learn the business. I turned in my notice at WFSB. My second sale was for a 1.2-million-dollar home, and I represented both buyer and seller. It was more money than I made in a year of driving to Hartford. It opened my eyes to a whole new level of income. Suddenly, I could see a bright future within reach if I worked hard and helped others. It was intoxicating.

But more than anything, I loved meeting people and working as an advocate to negotiate the best terms or coach a home seller to a full price offer. Each situation was different and it required thinking on your feet like I had done covering the news, but no bullet holes.

In five years' time, I was a top producer. I leased a sleek black Mercedes, an office space, and hired an assistant. I had a killer ad budget and quickly became addicted to the adrenaline rush of deals. I met many interesting people from NYC who ventured north for a country weekend home: artists, CEOs, celebrities, attorneys, publicists, and many others.

Real estate opened a world I had never known. At one conference at the Four Seasons in Beverly Hills, we toured several properties in excess of fifty million dollars and ended up at the Hilton's home for a cocktail event. Below us, a sea of lights sparkled against the Hollywood Hills. I met Kathy Hilton (this was pre-Paris fame) and chatted with her and her husband, Rick, over plates of delicate hors d'oeuvres that looked too pretty to eat. The chocolate even had gold on it.

Then the crash came.

The party was over.

It was humbling, but I emerged stronger. My embarrassment turned into scars. I was a survivor.

After 2010, I worked on rebuilding my real estate business. Once remarried, I enrolled in school full-time to finish my bachelor's degree. The day I stood on the stage, college diploma in hand, I thought back to all those years ago when I moved my stuff out of my dorm room at UMass. I had promised myself I would finish my degree and years later, I succeeded. I never gave up. I decided I would apply to law school. I knew it was a long shot.

I took the LSAT after studying for months. My score was not great, but I still filled out the applications and poured my energy into writing a personal essay detailing my accomplishments and struggles.

I called Mary.

"I will never get in," I said.

"Yes, you will. And you are trying. That means a lot. Look how far you have come! You are smart. You can do anything!"

I laughed. "What would I do without you?"

A few months later I got the email. The decision email.

I could not believe it. I was accepted to law school. I cried rivers of tears that day. I cried because it meant I was worthy. I cried because I had proven something to myself.

But I also cried because I knew I could not go to law school.

It was impossible.

I had to work to support our family. The kids needed me more than ever. There was no way I could do it all.

There have been a few times in my life I needed to set aside my dreams and focus on my personal commitments. Someday, my time would come. I had so many blessings in life that after I cried it out of my system, I found peace. I had so much to be grateful for.

Getting into law school was a huge accomplishment, but life had other plans for me. Another path opened at the same time. My managing broker, Carolyn, was a mentor, and I admired her greatly. She encouraged me in my real estate business and challenged me to grow.

We had dinner and I told her about law school and how I really wanted to help others. Turns out, a new role opened in management.

"You would be perfect," she said, and got me an interview with the CEO.

I officially became an assistant managing broker. Just like that, my life took a turn onto a new path.

STILL GRATEFUL

Ian and I sat doing bills on a Sunday, as was our routine. We were tight again. I took the job in management and was eager to learn the ropes, but it represented a large salary cut. Someday it would pay off. I hoped.

"We just have to eat out less," he said.

The numbers kept coming up short.

"I will have to earn more."

"You are doing great. Give it time," he hugged me. Ian was my rock. When I was in college, he took care of the kids. When I worked late, he made dinner. He even shopped for back-to-school supplies or nursed a sick child. He was my Superman.

"I appreciate you so much. And I love you," I told him.

"At least you have weekends with us now."

Although I was grateful for what we had, I was ready for more. I returned to my affirmations.

A few months later, a bigger job within the company became available, and I got a promotion. A noteworthy raise and we jumped to a new income bracket. That night, we opened a bottle of champagne and danced in our kitchen.

The next morning when I opened my eyes, I thought:

I am grateful for the kindness of others.

I am grateful for this opportunity to earn income for my family.

I am grateful for our warm house.

I am grateful for the food in our cabinets.

I am grateful for the health of my children.

I am grateful I am alive.

And butter.

Leading with Gratitude

The country road twisted and turned until I reached a gate. I admired the detailed wood and polished metal.

I rolled down my window and pressed the call box button.

A voice said "Welcome" and the gate opened slowly.

I followed the well-manicured driveway. The tree line parted to reveal a peek of the estate. "Nice," I said to myself as I finally pulled in front of the jaw-dropping stone mansion, complete with a magnificent turret, slate roof, and oversized windows. I grabbed my briefcase and headed toward the front door. Not only was this a well-known estate featured in local history books, but it was owned by one of the most influential families in the area. As the regional manager, I was going to the listing interview with one of my top agents.

A wave of gratitude washed over me. This was my life now. I was very blessed and found purpose in helping my agents realize their goals. This beautiful setting was just icing on the cake.

More often now I found myself inside a multimillion-dollar home with stunning details.

During the presentation (in which we met with family members and three attorneys), we fully articulated the power of our luxury real estate brand. We also connected by being what Patrick Lencioni refers to as "Humble, Hungry, Smart" (Lencioni 2016). If you ever want to know the secret sauce for success, it always comes back to these three traits.

My interpretation is humble: you admit to your mistakes, recognize you are not perfect, and temper the ego with a growth mindset; hungry: you want to succeed and be compensated for excellent performance, and you have ambition to go the extra mile for everyone around you; smart: you are "people smart," and can read a person or a room by asking questions and remain curious about everything.

I have had the honor of meeting some incredibly successful people. Some famous. Some titans in their industry. Being humble is one of the best personality traits you can have regardless of how smart or rich you are. Gratitude is the key to being humble. By constantly practicing the habit of grateful, you focus on all the blessings you have. Not only are grateful people happier but they are also a pleasure to be around because they appreciate you.

I have always tried to be Humble, Hungry, and Smart in everything I do. That day, we passed the interview and secured the multimillion-dollar listing. Shortly after, our agent sold the property for a record-breaking price. I was beyond proud of my team.

"You are crushing it," the CEO told me time and time again.

My role had grown and I oversaw six offices in multiple territories. My stats were off the charts. I won awards and made a great living. I was successful beyond what I thought possible. When I first started managing, I thought my role was numbers and procedures. Legal compliance. Profitability. I thought that I had to "make" people do things.

When you are a young female leader, you are constantly challenged. I had the experience of being on a construction site in which I made all the decisions, yet the builder turned to my junior male colleague.

"Hey buddy, she's the boss," he said to the builder.

"Wait, *you* are the boss? Aren't you a bit young?"

I smiled politely. "I prefer 'decision-maker.'"

Perhaps I needed to be more manly, I thought. I cut my hair short and bought boxy blazers. I tried to have an edge. Be all business. Facts and figures. Rules. Laws. I tried to be more aggressive. More assertive. I could be tough as steel. Let's face it, I could be mean as hell. I could be a total bitch. Being mean is easy.

But that never felt good.

I realized the key to leadership is love and compassion. Empathy. In the book *How to Win Friends and Influence People*, Dale Carnegie writes that the key to leadership is getting to know the personal lives of those you work with as a genuine human being. To care holistically (Carnegie 1998). You need to understand "the why" for working and what makes them tick. In other words, being "all business" with the agents I led was a mistake.

Perhaps I still felt unworthy. Perhaps a part of me wondered if I was good enough.

So I tried some new things.

I made an effort to slow down my conversations and ask more questions. I sought out mentors. I read books about how leadership worked. I became vulnerable. I no longer wanted to be an ice queen.

This was pivotal in my career because it gave me permission to be my authentic self and not hide my emotions in a blazer with shoulder pads. As women especially, we are taught we can't be emotional; we need to "put that away." But there is a balance. You can be professional and a leader and still care deeply.

One of my favorite agents was a famous fashion designer in his previous life. Ron always dressed impeccably and knew how to stage a house like no one else.

"Mama!" he would call me lovingly.

"Yes, dear?" I'd say.

"How are you today, Mama?" he would ask with a grin.

We both knew a true mama both took care of business and loved you at the same time.

Gratitude helped me soften and I became more curious about the people with whom I worked. I infused gratitude into my workday every moment possible. In my conversations with agents, I always started out by asking, "What are you grateful for today?" They softened and melted. They talked about their cat or their kids or their elderly parent. Some would tell me they were grateful they were alive or they were grateful for their health. This often led to a conversation about their life and what was most important to them.

One day my agent Ellen broke her wrist. She sat down at my desk and held her cast protectively. She hunched forward. Her body language looked defeated. A long, drawn-out sigh. "I can't do anything with a broken wrist," she said. "And I live alone, so it's been awful!"

"I am sorry to hear this. Do you need help with anything?"

"No, I'm fine." She looked anything but fine.

We continued the conversation on some real estate deals. I ended with, "Let me ask you a quick question, Ellen. What are you grateful for today? Is there anything good happening?"

She laughed sarcastically. Then a pause. "Gosh, I am so grateful for my health. Other than this wrist, I am healthy. I was taking my good health for granted. Do you know how hard it is to not be able to use your right hand?"

I looked at my hands and immediately felt grateful.

"Thanks for reminding me to be grateful for my health!" I said.

She smiled and we talked for a few more minutes.

When I made this change, I felt more confident. I had better relationships with my staff. I asked them what they were grateful for. I took time to learn about their lives, what made them tick. I loved my people and that in return made me love my job for so much more than a paycheck.

I also learned having a growth mindset and why that is crucial. I am an eternal student of many things, but the one thing I love to study is the power of gratitude. When I look back at my life, I see it as a lifeline that got me through the tough times. But gratitude also ran into my future; a strong arrow guiding me forward.

THE NINJA EFFECT

Everything was perfect. Or so I thought.

There was an itch in me.

I had plateaued in my climb. Having overcome my divorce and financial struggles, I was in a place I had longed for, but I still wanted more. I was stuck. Something was missing.

In real estate, I kept hearing about "Ninja." I admit the very name of it made me roll my eyes. I was not the "salesy" *rah rah* type.

I learned when you keep hearing the same suggestion, it is often a sign from the universe. So after five more people suggested Ninja to me, I finally I bought the book by Larry Kendall called *Ninja Selling*.

It rocked my world.

Kendall's first chapter begins with energy. How in sales, we need to consciously focus on our personal energy. The high and low positive energy quadrants are where we should dwell, and gratitude is one of the ways we can get there (Kendall 2017).

I could not put the book down. Kendall's entire book is centered on service and giving value. I registered for an in-person class in Fort Collins, Colorado, called an "Installation" (check out NinjaSelling.com). I had to meet him.

I took a three-day leadership course at The Group's office. I was suddenly immersed in Kendall's world, and his teachings encompassed some of the best scholars in positive thinking (Dweck, Williamson, Sperry, and more) and how to identify and move past self-limiting beliefs. You could attract whatever you want with an abundance mindset.

But for me, the morning routine in *Ninja Selling* (Kendall 2017) was perhaps the most valuable:

- Gratitudes
- Affirmations
- Two note cards a day
- Read something positive

My "two notes a day" morphed into notes of gratitude. I told others why I was grateful for them. It was therapeutic. This also reminded me of the letters Mary and I sent to each other and how that deepened our friendship over time.

Often someone called me to thank me for my note. They would then tell me I had "made their day" or the note came to them in a time when they were down or depressed. This led to a feeling best described as "a spark of kindness." A warm and fuzzy sense of purpose, knowing I had touched someone and made them feel special.

Our words have power. When you write your words and send them, they have a huge impact.

Larry Kendall helped me to understand gratitude on a deeper level. He inspired me to become a student of gratitude. This means I continue to read books, watch lectures, and stay curious.

I am eternally grateful.

RAISE A HAND (IN GRATITUDE)

The hotel is large and majestic. It greets you when you arrive with polished door handles, an army of staff who welcome you, and just beyond the high, perfectly coiffed green hedges there is, of course, the Atlantic Ocean. And palm trees. You can't forget the palm trees.

I was at The Breakers for a real estate leadership conference. I felt like the luckiest girl in the world as I met CEOs and top executives of the number one luxury real estate brand in the country. There is something special about staying at a luxurious hotel and walking the grounds with the deep blue Atlantic Ocean churning as a backdrop. Each morning I focused on feeling grateful for this gift.

I earned my spot by hitting several milestones. The reward went further than the hotel stay—it allowed me the chance to get into a room with the top leaders for our global brand. I wanted to meet them.

After the main session ended, I spotted our new COO and took a place in line to introduce myself. She was young, super intelligent, and motivational. In a way, I wanted to be her.

"Hi, I wanted to introduce myself," I said and shook her hand.

We chatted and I told her how much I enjoyed her speech and how grateful I was to see a young female leader in her position. "You are an inspiration!"

"Leaders like you are the inspiration," she said.

Months later she invited me to host a national webinar for our entire company. The best part was that I got to interview many top managers and leaders and ask them how they were so successful. What I learned was invaluable.

I think my daily habit of gratitude helped me to build confidence. You see, by focusing on others, I took the focus off myself. When you are nervous about how you will look or sound, or if you belong, just focus on others. It works every time: focus on helping others and being grateful for them.

Gratitude has not only been a mirror for my soul, but it has been the anchor in my career.

Habit #3—Writing Notes of Gratitude

- Write handwritten notes of gratitude and send them in the mail.

- Aim for five to seven a week, or more if you wish.

- Tell others why you are grateful for them.

- Use the enclosed writing prompts.

A handwritten note of gratitude is extremely powerful and has long-reaching impact. Not only does it provide a benefit to the one penning the letter (by practicing gratitude), but the recipient also has the benefit of feeling appreciated.

Imagine you get your mail and amongst the bills there is a handwritten envelope addressed to you. It's from a friend. You open it and read something inside that tells you how grateful your friend is for you, and how much you have positively impacted them. In that moment, it's like the envelope contained a warm hug. You feel uplifted. Special. Your entire day feels lighter. Happier.

Writing notes of gratitude to others is a big part of your gratitude habit. When you tell someone how much you appreciate them, you acknowledge they are important. They matter. They have made a difference. One of the most beautiful feelings in life is being appreciated. Receiving such a note is one of the best gifts you can get.

The study "Letters of Gratitude: Further Evidence for Author Benefits" assessed the health benefits of notes of gratitude. The researchers found that writing as few as three weekly thank you notes improved life satisfaction, increased happy feelings, and reduced symptoms of depression (Toepfer, Cichy, and Peters 2012).

I personally have collected past notes and letters and they are a constant source of encouragement; something tangible to save and cherish. They continue to bring joy long after they are received. If a person pops into your mind, this can be the universe telling you to reach out. Take this cue and call, text, or write them a gratitude note.

It's easy to say, "I was just thinking about you," or, "You popped into my mind and I wanted to reach out to you."

Let's consider some of the reasons to send a note of gratitude to others:

- Perhaps you recall a beautiful memory of someone from your past.

- It is a family member/friend's special day and you feel especially grateful for them.

- Perhaps someone demonstrates an act of kindness to you or to others.

- Perhaps you meet someone and they make an impression on you.

These are all great reasons to send a note of gratitude. If you have ever had the devastating experience of losing someone unexpectedly, you may have experienced regret. You may have wished you told them how important they were to you while they were still alive. Make a pledge to yourself that you will let everyone know how much you care. Don't wait.

Gratitude will strengthen your relationships. Notes to your loved ones, friends, and colleagues all become part of your routine. This creates an outpouring of love, kindness, and gratitude. Together we can make the world a better place by choosing to focus on being grateful and sharing with others.

In the next pages you will find instructions and templates for sending notes of gratitude. This is the perfect addition to your daily gratitude habit of waking up and thinking about what you are grateful for. Aim to send a pile of notes at least once a week or consider sending a note of gratitude every day—more challenging, but highly rewarding!

In addition to having a goal of how many notes a week you will send, be sure to get yourself set up so you have everything you need handy.

- You will need note cards with envelopes, stamps, or print-at-home postage, and a few good pens. Have fun with this and get notes/pens you enjoy.

- Simple note cards are best. Buy in bulk. I have a box full of stationery and supplies.

- You will also need to start collecting mailing addresses. You can email, text, or direct message on social media to ask for someone's mailing address.

- Simply say, "Can you share your mailing address with me so I can send you a note?" You can also look them up online or check their email signature for a mailing address.

- Google Contacts works well for storing addresses or you can create an Excel spreadsheet. There are also several other platforms you can check out. Create a system that works best for you.

- It is helpful to keep track when you send someone a note. I have an ongoing list of who I want to write to and I check off their name. You can even take a picture of the note you write and save it to your camera roll in an album marked "gratitudes."

- My friend Ben gave me a great tip: he writes two notes every day. He always addresses the envelopes of the next day's batch and leaves them on his desk so they are waiting for him. Ben says addressing the card is the hardest part for him, so this makes it a breeze to write his notes.

A HELPFUL EXERCISE (THE WARM UP)

Find a quiet space. Close your eyes for a moment and take a few deep breaths and relax. Now concentrate on your heart and how full it is with thanks. Feel thankfulness that you are alive and are here on Earth with another full day to *live*. Take a few deep breaths in and out and feel the absolute joy of being alive.

START WRITING

Grab a blank piece of paper so you can make a list of people you wish to thank. Take some time and think about all the wonderful people who have made you feel loved; people who showed you kindness, big or small.

As people come to mind, jot them down. Spend as much time as you need thinking of people you appreciate.

Fill the page with names. Don't self-edit. Just write down as many names as you can. Pick the first person you want to write a note to. Grab scrap paper to write out your note as a draft. This allows you to write freely, and if you make a mistake, you won't ruin your card. Spend some time on your note. Remember, gratitude works best when you are *specific*.

Tell them why you are grateful for them and then elaborate. The more details, the better.

Start with a greeting like "Dear Diane." Begin by identifying your connection or the last time you saw or spoke to them, if appropriate. If you have not met, acknowledge why you are writing. Then be sure to tell them you are grateful for them and why.

Here is an example:

Dear Jack,

Thank you for connecting with me last week. I am very grateful you spent time with me discussing my career plans. It means a lot to me to have someone in my corner, cheering me on. Your positive energy and encouragement have helped me to believe in myself. Your advice is really appreciated.

With gratitude,

Kristine

Need some help getting started? Try using these writing prompts and sentence starters.

WRITING PROMPTS AND INSPIRATION

- Today, I am thinking of you and how grateful I am for...

- You are a person I am grateful for. I especially want to share...

- I am writing to express my gratitude for...

- I really appreciate...

- Thank you for always being someone I...

- I just want to thank you for taking the time to...

- Thank you for taking the time to...

- I want you to know how much I appreciate...

- I am grateful for...

- Thank you for being in my life. You are/have been a blessing to me because...

- Thank you for being the person who...

- You have changed my life with your...

- I sincerely appreciate the way that you...

- You are such an inspiration. I wanted to acknowledge...

- You should know how amazing you are.

- I am so humbled and grateful.

- Wow! You have made an impact.

- I felt compelled to tell you how much I respect and admire you.

- Sometimes, it's the simple things that touch us the most.

- Thank you for your advice on...

- Your kindness makes the world a better place.

- You are a bright light of positivity.

- Your thoughtfulness is a gift.

- I am impressed by all that you have given.

- Your constant support means the world to me and I appreciate you.

- The _____ you made were fabulous. Your kindness and talent are appreciated

- You continue to inspire and amaze me. I'm touched beyond words.

- You have made a difference.

NOTES OF GRATITUDE

Utilize any of the form letters below. Add in your own thoughts as you like:

Dear ___,

I am so happy we connected. I appreciate your kind words and positivity.

Thank you for your time. I am grateful.

Sincerely, your name

Dear ___,

I was just thinking of you and want you to know how much I appreciate you. You are such a positive force in my life. Thank you for all you do for me.

I am grateful for you.

With gratitude, your name

Dear ___,

I wanted to write you a note to thank you for being such an amazing friend. I cherish our friendship and am grateful to have you in my life.

Thank you for always being there for me.

With appreciation, your name

Dear ___,

I am so happy we have met and look forward to getting to know you.

Thank you for the inspiration and kind words.

Sincerely, your name

Dear ___,

I am excited that we have connected.

Thanks for taking the time to chat. I appreciate you.

Love, your name

Dear ___,

I wanted to take a moment to recognize your positive contributions and constant support.

I am grateful to have the privilege of working with you.

With much appreciation, your name

Dear ___,

I just want to take a moment to let you know how much I appreciate you.

Your kindness is a gift and I am grateful for you.

Many thanks.

With gratitude, your name

Dear ___,

Thank you for all you do. You are a gift to the world.

With deep appreciation and gratitude.

Love, your name

One of the best parts of writing notes to others is the special rush you get when they thank you.

Most people respond with absolute delight and call or text you and thank you for your note.

Others may not acknowledge it and that's okay. What matters is you took the time to write your gratitude and send it. You should always give a gift without expectation of a thank you.

Consider hand-delivering a note of gratitude instead of mailing it or even reading it out loud in person to the recipient if it is appropriate. The length of your note is your personal choice and may be different depending on the circumstance.

Here are some fun people to send a note of gratitude to:

- Family and friends

- Teachers or school staff

- Doctors

- Pet groomers

- Coffee baristas

- Favorite restaurant owner or server postal worker

- Town hall employees

- UPS/Amazon delivery workers

- Dentists and/or hygienists

- Receptionists

- Hairstylists/barbers

- Nail/spa technicians

- Co-workers

- Office staff at your workplace accountant

- Coaches

- Gym attendants/trainers

- Babysitters

- Mentors

- Authors of your favorite books

- Friends on social media

- Photographers

- Nurses

- Firefighters/police or first responders

- Elderly relatives

- Neighbors

- Networking group

- Pastors or priests

- Church friends

- Therapists/social workers

PRO TIPS

- Have a gratitude playlist of inspirational music. Listen while you are writing or to get into a positive mindset.

- Keep looking for opportunities to thank others with a note of gratitude.

- You can keep names you wish to write to in a journal or even use the "notes" application on your phone/computer. I add names to my daily "to do" list.

- Remember to send notes weekly or daily as part of your commitment to a habit of gratitude.

- Keep it going.

THE BOX OF GRATITUDE

Check out BoxofGratitude.com and buy a kit with everything you need to get started.

The Grateful Parent

Potty training and teenagers. Some of my best work.

As a mom of four, there were many nights I awoke startled by a tiny hand, vomiting, or a screaming child. Parenthood is twenty-four seven and not for the faint of heart. Gratitude helped me to be a better parent: more patient and more loving.

I still remember when the kids were young and I worked full-time while finishing my college degree. Liam, our youngest, was in diapers and Triston was getting his license.

As part of my graduation project, I wrote a collection of essays on motherhood:

> I am a mother of four children. Daily, I run a household, keep myself looking fit, and work a "day job." I own and use a Crock-Pot. Like Grace Paley, I write at the kitchen table while permission slips, waiting dishes, and sippy cups surround me. Children screaming, fighting, or shitting their pants. In the style of Virginia Woolf, "a room of one's own" seems heavenly, but also as unrealistic as winning the lottery.

Our house was always bustling and I struggled to stay in balance with the demands of school, sports schedules, friends, birthdays, and dentist and doctor appointments, all while having a career and trying to have my own life. It was exhausting.

But it does not last forever. That is the thing about motherhood: when you are in the thick of carpooling, a messy house, freezing at soccer games, and the constant whirlwind, it is about getting through it without losing your temper or running away. Someday, the kids will grow up and you will miss it. Terribly.

When Triston moved out of the house to go to college, it really hit me. Not only had he grown like a weed and sprouted big shoulders and facial hair, but he became a man. In my mind, he will always be four years old in the back seat of my car singing Lenny Kravitz, with a striped shirt I picked out and his bowl-cut blond hair.

It goes by fast. People always warned me, but until one flies the nest, you don't understand.

I am so grateful for the privilege of being a parent and the mom of four special humans, all gifted in their own way. I have learned so much as a mom and have been filled with such love.

I think I held onto the other three even tighter after Triston moved out. Each day, when I say my gratitudes, I am grateful for my children. I think this has made me a better mother.

Then it was Jacob's turn and in the blink of an eye, he was a strapping young man with a full head of curly hair and five o'clock shadow. We shared a mutual love for the soundtrack of

Hamilton, and anytime we were in a car together, we blasted it and sang together. As a surprise, I took him to NYC to see the show live. It was a memory we will never forget.

Jacob's path was different, and he chose to attend a private boarding school. Every Friday, I drove to his campus and collected his laundry. I washed and pressed his khakis and button-down shirts. I clung to his clothes and it made me happy to know there was still a part of him at home, that there was something I could still do for him even though he lived on campus.

When your child boards at school, it is a different high school experience entirely. I was so thankful for Jacob's "house mother," Mrs. Jordan. She called and updated me and soothed my anxiety. In time, she and Jacob became very close. She invited him to hang out with her family, and she directed him in various stage productions at school. When things got tough, she advocated for him. Words can't express my gratitude toward Mrs. Jordan. She changed the course of his life with her kindness.

After Jacob graduated, I called the many teachers who helped him and I personally thanked each one. I was so grateful for the support he received and all he had achieved. The conversations left me tearful. There is nothing like a mother's gratitude.

My in-laws retired around the time we had Liam. They watched him from when he was a baby through elementary school. It became obvious to me the reason I had a demanding career was partly due to their help. Even during a snowstorm, when school was cancelled, or if he was sick, they always pitched in. I wrote them a note of gratitude and put it in the mail. It was the best gift I could think of. A heartfelt thank you.

If you have a child, can you look for a way to thank those around them? Your pediatrician, teacher, the grandparents, childcare, etc. Better yet, teach your children to use gratitude.

At the dinner/breakfast table, take turns and share one thing you are grateful for. This is a fun way to share a daily gratitude with your children and teach them your new superpower.

TOO SOON

It was a Monday morning and I was up early on the elliptical in our finished basement. Getting in a thirty-minute workout before I started my workday helped reset my mind. It was deep COVID-19 and the world had a pause button on its big blue globe. It had stopped spinning, just waiting for God (or anyone really) to hit the play button again. And so we waited.

My phone went off. My friend texted me. *Did you see the news? Litchfield teenagers in car crash.*

I texted back. *No. Where did you see it?*

She sent me the link and the words filled my screen: "Litchfield Car Crash. Multiple victims."

My daughter was a junior at Litchfield High and there were only sixty kids in her class. Surely, we probably knew them. I stopped my workout and went upstairs to her room and knocked. No answer.

I opened the door and saw she was not in her bed. Panic set in.

"*Amelia!*" I said louder and then heard the toilet flush and realized she was in the bathroom. Thank god.

"Honey, there has been an accident. Have you heard?"

"What?" she asked in her teenage constantly annoyed voice. "I'm sleeping."

"There was an accident." I read her the headline.

She grabbed her phone. "I hope it was not Matt and those guys. I know they were out late last night and..."

The next hour was painful. She got texts and Snapchats. We still didn't know much. Dylan, Matt, and Thomas were in the car and two others. I sat in my sweaty, now-cold gym clothes and tried to comfort/not smother her.

"Two have passed away," she said, reading a text.

"What? Oh my god...who?" I asked, terrified of the answer.

"I don't know." Then, "No one knows."

I felt numb and afraid. I called in sick and cancelled my Zooms. My daughter didn't "log into" school. A group of her friends gathered and she got dressed to go join them. I wanted to keep her in this room, keep her safe forever, but I realized this is an impossible wish.

Our world changed when she texts me their names. *Thomas.* Then *Matt.*

I dropped to the ground and screamed. It's a primal cry when you learn of something that just can't be real. I wished for a way to undo the horrible news and go back in time.

I remembered lunch with his mom, Dawn, not long ago. Amelia had a crush on Matt in middle school and they were fast friends over the last five years. Dawn also sold real estate and we ate our Cobb salads in our normal town pub on a normal Wednesday in a normal small town. We talked about real estate, and, of course, Amelia and Matt. They shared English and a few other classes.

"Does he give you problems?" I asked. "Talking back?"

"No. Not Matt. He is so easy," she said and smiled. I could tell how much she loved him. "He eats everything. He is always hungry!" We laughed.

Matt was six feet tall, gorgeous, and had a wicked sense of humor. My daughter, also blond and blue-eyed, often told me, "Mom, people think we are related." She cheered. He led the basketball team. Matt was always there to comfort her after breakups or arguments with a friend. He was a voice of reason.

I heard the door open and Amelia ran to me. "I can't believe he's gone, Mom." We cried together and I stroked her hair. Every time I thought of his mom, I felt sick.

Details slowly emerged. Our small community was shocked and horrified all at once. The funeral was outside. Even though it was deep COVID-19, there was a need to gather and so we all did. My daughter stood with her friends and they shook with sobs, holding each other in the green grass. I remember the preacher said a few words and I stood with clumps of parents, knowing we all wanted to wake up from a bad dream; this could not be real.

I learned more about Matt. He was a prankster and loved jokes. He loved his friends and was kind. A leader. People looked up to him. He loved to laugh. He volunteered at the local fire station. He wanted to go to college, maybe California. He was a bright shining star. Charismatic. Caring.

But most importantly, he was a friend to my daughter every time she needed him. I am grateful for his kindness. He left a big imprint on her heart. To this day, she carries his memory with her. His family set up a scholarship fund in memory of Matt to help others. For information, visit MatthewRousseauAim-ForTheStarsFundraiser.com

When you are close to a tragedy, it seeps into your skin and alters everything. For my daughter, she became an adult overnight. The pain of loss crept up and slapped her often. Tears and disbelief. Anger. And longing. For my daughter, high school had morphed into something dark and scary. First with COVID-19, which changed everything and shut down her world, then with the loss of two friends and the heaviness that settled around her friends like fog.

A year later, we were away for my birthday in Rhode Island. We were on the deck of a house we rented after dinner. We sat in darkness and candles. The night sky above us was full of stars. Our family talked about friends and funny stories. We laughed and ate cake. I avoided the frosting.

Amelia said out of nowhere, "I miss Matt so much." She started to cry. I hugged her, our heads bumping through our hoodies, and I held her tight because I was suddenly aware, as I had been each day since he passed, how precious life was and how much of a gift it was to hold your child; how blessed I was to have a daughter and how much I needed to remember this gift and never take it for granted.

I looked up at the stars.

My daughter shook as she cried. My heart broke.

"I know, honey. It's okay to be sad. It's okay to miss him."

She said, "I really thought I would marry him someday."

Just over her shoulder, I saw a fast, shooting star.

The Road to Gratitude: A Map

"Remember this, that very little is needed to make a happy life."

—MARCUS AURELIUS

This year marks the tenth anniversary of the *World Happiness Report*, which uses global survey data to report how people evaluate their own happiness in more than 150 countries. You can read it at WorldHappiness.report.

Interestingly, the *World Happiness Report* published in 2022 reveals a "bright light in dark times." The aftermath of the pandemic brought not only pain and suffering but also an increase in social support and benevolence. More than ever, happiness is an area of focus and importance for those surveyed (World Happiness Report 2022).

But what is happiness?

Is it a moment or a good day? Is it an emotion or state of being? Do you regard yourself as "happy"? What would your perfect day look like? Can you take a moment and jot that down? Now, if you could repeat that day over and over for a hundred years, would that equate a life of happiness?

The term "positive psychology" has been linked to happiness. The definition of positive psychology is "the scientific study of what makes life most worth living" (Peterson 2008).

In an article for PsychologyToday.com, Courtney Ackerman states, "The practice of positive psychology focuses on the positive events and influences in life, including:

1. Positive experiences (like happiness, joy, inspiration, and love).

2. Positive states (like gratitude, resilience, and compassion).

3. Positive institutions (applying positive principles within entire organizations and institutions)" (Ackerman 2018).

Reach into the pocket of the positive psychology movement and you are sure to grab a handful of gratitude. Focus on seeing the world in a rose-tinted light. Gratitude is the easiest tool to get you there. As positive psychology pioneer Martin Seligman said on *Larry King Live*, "Grateful people are happier" (Smith 2018).

I was recently at a leadership summit and having lunch with some colleagues. There was a group of about eight of us sitting at a round table, eating salads and talking about our families. Someone asked Linda how her husband was doing. They both worked in real estate for many years and had a passion for helping others succeed. Dick, her husband, retired years ago and his health had been declining.

"It's not good," Linda said. You could see sadness in her eyes and she looked down at the table.

"I am so sorry," someone offered.

"His memory is just not there anymore. And I can't leave him alone. Dick served in the navy; he was an officer. He can tell you the layout of ships and every detail of all he did while serving down to the minute detail, but he can't remember the names of family members who visit. He doesn't recognize them."

Many of us at the table knew Dick, so this was troubling news.

"That is just awful, Linda."

"My sister stays with him during the day when I go to work. I don't know what I would do without her. And thankfully, our company understands when I adjust my hours. Our CEO is very supportive." I could sense the weight on her shoulders, and it was obvious how hard this was for her. More than anything, the love she had for her husband was evident.

Then she said, "But I am so grateful I have my job. Not only am I grateful for the income, but I love going to the office and helping so many people. Like one of our up-and-coming stars in the office. I am so grateful my boss is supportive of my situation. And I am so, so grateful my sister will come over every day and stay with Dick when I must leave the house. She is so giving. I am just so grateful. And blessed. She is such a gift."

Linda's entire demeanor changed. In that moment, she used gratitude to lift herself back up. She shared with our entire table a twist of perception. By focusing (even in this hard time) on gratitude and the blessings around her, she shifted into a positive mindset.

"You are very lucky," I said, "to have that support."

She nodded and smiled.

"And we just got the cutest cat. She is a ball of energy and has such a personality. But it's funny because Dick thinks we have several cats. He will say, 'That other cat went under the bed,' and then a few minutes later he will say, 'The other cat is looking for a treat.'" Linda laughed. "You have to laugh at this stuff sometimes. You just have to find the humor in life and smile."

In that moment, I was grateful for Linda. Not only for her strength, but how she reminded me of my blessings by recounting hers.

Robert Emmons is the world's leading expert on gratitude. In his book *Thanks! How the New Science of Gratitude Can Make You Happier*, Emmons writes that gratitude has one of the strongest indicators to mental health and satisfaction of life than any other personality trait (Emmons 2007). He catalogues his findings on his own (and others') research on the benefits of a regular practice of gratitude.

Specifically, a gratitude journal can be a helpful tool to help track and memorialize the many things for which you are grateful. There are countless studies that connect keeping a gratitude journal or "writing down what you are grateful for daily" to practice the habit of gratitude and stay in a positive mindset. Oprah Winfrey considers "gratitude to be a spiritual practice" and recently shared her latest entries in her gratitude journal with *Oprah Daily* writer Adrienne Farr:

"Savoring a raspberry sorbet. The color of a maple leaf changing. A three-dog night, when all the pups are snuggled in bed"
—OPRAH WINFREY (FARR 2022).

The very simple things in life can be the most beautiful. Being grateful for these tiny moments of joy can help us in our quest for happiness. Feeling good. Seeing the world more clearly.

In fact, scientists studying positive psychology found a one-time act of thoughtful gratitude produced an immediate 10 percent increase in happiness and 35 percent reduction in depressive symptoms. The happy effects disappeared within three to six months which shows gratitude is a habit to be repeated to deliver results (Seligman 2005).

What if more gratitude could help you feel happier by changing the lens through which you see the world? What if a habit of grateful is like a pair of rose-tinted glasses you can slip on?

A study published in the *Journal of Neuroscience* in 2009 showed that "our moods could change how our visual cortex operates" (Schmitz 2009). Using Functional Magnetic Resonance Imaging (fMRI) technology, researchers found subjects with a positive mindset could take in more visual information and saw more detail in imagery. The subjects with more negative moods had more limited perception (Schmitz 2009).

By reviewing the fMRI data, the scientists determined that the positively primed subjects had greater stimulation in the brain's parahippocampal cortex: responsible for "memory formation and high-level visual processing," as explained by the National Center for Biotechnology Information (Woods 2021).

Our disposition does affect how we see and what we notice around us. With this research, it's apparent when we are happy, we see the world around us more clearly. Those rose-tinted glasses of gratitude help you expand your awareness and not miss things around you.

TIP:
Here is an exercise for when something is bothering you and you need to be reminded of the positive elements that exist, even in the hardest situations:

Take out a piece of paper and draw a line down the middle. On the left side, write down the negative components to a situation. Now, on the right-hand column, next to each negative, try to find a positive attribute. When you are done, recognize the growth in your situation by embracing the positives. Each time you are drawn to the problems or negative aspects, remind yourself that with each negative, there is positive.

Find the positive. Use gratitude. It is a road map to your destination.

SCARCITY VS. ABUNDANCE

Scarcity is the mindset that you do not have enough. It is the voice whispering "danger" or "doom."

Are you predisposed to a scarcity or negative mindset? We all are to some extent, and our DNA is laced with the goods to survive. Our "caveman brain" is always scanning for danger. The freeze-flight-fight response is a set of evolutionary adaptations increasing the chances of survival in threatening situations. "Consciously or unconsciously appraising an event as dangerous triggers an automatic defense cascade of physiological and cognitive responses that prepare the individual to freeze, flee, or fight" (Kozlowska Walker McLean Carrive 2015).

Fast forward to modern day and there is a plethora of stimulation. It's the electric jolt of your smart watch. It's the adrenaline rush beginning when you pick up your blue glowing screen and start scrolling. News, texts, politics, headlines, and social media: the connectivity is twenty-four seven.

It's a lot.

In a world of social media sharing, it is also easy to see what you do not have. Never have we had these windows into the personal lives of others so readily accessible to us and to our children. You can't help but look at fancy cars, fancy things, fancy people and feel...well...so average.

I still remember when I was going through my divorce and the real estate market was in full meltdown during the crash of 2008. I was at the grocery store with twenty dollars. I remember eyeing other people's grocery carts overloaded with food. Steaks and seafood and all kinds of produce just piled up rolling past me, as if to show me what I could not have.

I thought, *Why me? Why did I not have a full cart?* I was angry. But the anger just made it worse. Why? Because I put myself in a victim mindset.

The opposite of scarcity is abundance. A positive mindset. There is enough for everyone, and especially for you.

As Dr. Rick Hanson states so eloquently:

> For our hunter-gatherer ancestors, [...] the biological inclination to feel threatened and react served them well. It kept them alive in extreme environments, and allowed them to pass their genes on to us, who are less well-served today by the inclination to register and react to whatever threatens us or causes discomfort. In fact, this hard-wired tendency is the cause of many emotional, physical, and psychological problems, some large, many small. Gratitude, the experience of what is good in one's life, even abundantly good, is a powerful and direct antidote to thoughts and feelings of being threatened. (Hanson 2007)

TIP:
If you use social media, pay attention to what you are "following." Make sure you have "liked" some thought leaders in the space of positive thinking, gratitude, abundance, and happiness. For each minute I read regular news, I also make sure to read good news from sources like GoodNewsNetwork.org.

You can also follow hashtags like "gratitude," "happiness," and "positive thinking" to help shape your social feed. Unfriend toxic people who are negative or spew hate. Remember, what you feed into your mind and the people you surround yourself with will directly impact your thoughts and feelings.

Surround yourself with gratitude enthusiasts. Share your love of being grateful. If you are lucky like me, you will find there are many devoted to this practice.

Find the gratitude lovers!

THE CITY OF LIGHT

We landed, tired from the transatlantic haul. Soon, Ian and I were snuggled in the back of a car taking in the sights of Paris, "the City of Light." It was our anniversary trip.

"It looks like a movie set," I whispered.

"It does," he said, putting his hand on my knee.

Everywhere we looked, we saw beauty. The exquisite stone buildings complete with intricate carvings and balconies. Oversized doors with etched glass and patterns of bent iron. Carved doors. Fountains. Stone roads with tiny fences. Even small signs written in French were intricate. Romantic.

After check-in and a quick nap, we headed outside to find our way to the Seine.

"Look!"

I looked up and there it was: the Eiffel Tower. It was lit up with a million small lights all sparkling and shining like electric glitter.

"Magnificent!" I said.

It was a moment, and I grabbed his hand and we kissed.

Shortly after, we floated down the Seine on an open river boat. He popped a tiny bottle of champagne and we toasted each other with plastic cups. Famous buildings and bridges floated by, lit up like a show. The Notre-Dame Cathedral, the Conciergerie, and the Eiffel Tower again. I would never tire of staring at it.

I had a million new gratitudes. Each moment was a wonderful surprise.

The next few days were a blur of joy with one moment of magic after the next.

We walked through the Musée d'Orsay, taking in the art until we found ourselves cradled against the gigantic clock in the tower. We stepped into it and looked at the city below. Pure awe. We saw the Van Goghs, of course, with his use of color and blue and gold and green. His work spoke to my soul. Another day at the Louvre. We stood in front of the *Mona Lisa*. A bucket list moment.

We roamed Paris again, St. Germain, and the wobbly hills of Montmartre. We stumbled into a pastry shop and got a peach raspberry tart that was one of the best things I had ever tasted. And *the bread*. It was insane.

I loved watching Parisians sip coffee and look effortlessly cool. We sat outside at bistro tables drinking wine, facing the street. I saw a thin, stylish girl in her twenties eating a baguette whole like a churro. "Everyone eats bread here!" I said happily.

"My kind of place," Ian said.

Walking in the city, bundled up in sweaters and scarves, I clung to him in the way I can only describe as "happy wife." The night of our anniversary, he booked a fancy restaurant. We sat at a candlelit table holding hands.

"Remember Newport?" I asked

"Remember ten thousand waves?" he said.

We laughed and traded our favorite places in the world we had been together.

"Paris is my new favorite, though," he said. "I can't imagine being in Paris with anyone but you."

"Agree," I said, toasting us. "To us. It's been a long road."

"And I have loved every minute."

Our waiter was a young kid, polite and nice.

"Do you have plans tonight for drinks after dinner?" he asked.

"We heard there is a cool nightclub not far from here. It's kind of underground," Ian said.

"Ah, yes. You have to know how to find it. I take you there?" he said in his thick accent.

"Awesome," Ian said, slipping him a twenty.

Later that night, our waiter grabbed his coat and walked us down the street a few blocks. It was a deserted street. I looked at Ian questioningly. "It's fine," he whispered.

The waiter approached a warehouse and knocked.

The door opened and a bouncer peered out. They spoke in French and said something about "Americans."

The bouncer welcomed us in. "Bonsoir."

Inside, it was a dimly lit, happening nightclub with library shelves, books, cozy seating everywhere, and a huge bar. The ceiling soared upward and there was a staircase to other levels with balconies. Super hip kids and some thirty-somethings (like us) milled around.

We got a fun drink and found a spot to take it all in.

"This is so cool!" I said.

A DJ was setting up. "I wonder what they will play?" I asked. "Electro?"

"I hope not," Ian said.

The music started. It was old-school '90s rap. We looked at each other and cracked up. All around us, the French sang Snoop

Dogg and Notorious B.I.G. with thick accents. "This is my jam!" I said, dancing in my seat.

"Americans, cool," the guy next to us said.

We cheered him and laughed.

We sang along to the music (we knew all the words) and I took a mental photograph to never forget that moment. How grateful I was. Not just for Paris, and butter, but for the love of my life next to me. I needed to cherish every moment.

What we didn't know was that the entire world would soon be flipped upside down.

COVID-19 and Gratitude

To look back at the way COVID-19 affected us is both nause-ating and confounding.

Everyone has their own perspective, touched by its long-reach-ing, creepy tentacles. In 2022, I finally contracted the virus. It had been hovering like some strange angel of death or particle mass of germs in the air for three years. Vaccinated and boosted, it finally made its way into my lungs. After countless negative tests, two lines lit up on the white stick and I was shocked/not so shocked. You can only avoid it for so long.

But actually contracting COVID-19 was not the majority of my experience.

In 2019, when it first emerged, COVID-19 brought:

1. The unknown
2. Netflix binging
3. Fear
4. Worldwide shutdown
5. Zoomaphoria
6. The Great Migration

The world suddenly changed. Masks. Hand sanitizer. Banks closed lobbies. It was eerie in the beginning how things just *shut down*. We cancelled vacations. We stopped eating out. We "sheltered in place."

I found myself feeling very grateful for my husband, our house (with a finished basement and four bedrooms), and the fact we were both fully employed. Even if real estate took a nosedive, with two incomes, I knew we would be financially stable.

Many others were not so lucky.

It changed our perspective on the world and, perhaps even harder to watch, the experience of our children in their formative years. Suddenly we were all at home. School was online. Masks hid faces. No more visiting friends or seeing extended family. Weekends were like weekdays with less Zoom. Sanitizing wipes. Lines at the grocery store. Just weird.

My daughter's last two years of high school became sad. No cheerleading. No dances. No homecoming. My youngest cried when we learned school might remain online indefinitely. "It's just not the same," he said, tears streaming down his face. He was nine. The SATs kept getting cancelled. My second eldest could not get an internship. My parents could not attend his graduation.

In the beginning, fear of the unknown was rampant. I could not sleep, so I drank a lot of wine at night and watched Netflix and worked from home in the upstairs office. My husband worked on the kitchen island and our youngest at the dining room table. Amelia was in her room mostly or with friends. Even letting our sixteen-year-old be with friends was a debate. Was it safe?

A family member was diagnosed with cancer just before coronavirus broke. We could wave to her from the windows, stand in the driveway (socially distanced and with masks), but we could not hug her.

All the rules and protocols of society changed overnight. I was both spooked and astonished by how quickly people in general adapted to these new "rules" and how the economy shut off like a big switch. Friends of ours in the restaurant business suddenly found themselves shutdown; something I could have never even conceived. Businesses folded. People lost everything.

Having gone through the downturn of 2009, I was totally paranoid. But thankfully we had worked hard, had savings, and then the real estate market rebounded.

My entire day transformed into online meetings. *Zoom, Zoom, Zoom.* One after another. We banded together and formed new online communities. I connected with thousands of realtors on Zoom and social media. Together, we illuminated a path forward.

After a few weeks of self-medicating with wine, chips, and Netflix at night, I knew I needed to refocus on the positive. No matter what, there is opportunity in every situation. There is a choice: freeze (cease action and ignore opportunity) or take action (seek out opportunity). I vowed to concentrate on the positive things now possible in this new world—things like connecting with others all over the country and creating new ways for my team to conduct business.

I surrounded myself with books on mindset and positivity and made it a focus to study and not get distracted by fear. I doubled down on affirmations and gratitude, and stopped drinking wine at night (for a few months).

I decided early mornings would become my private time to concentrate on myself and I began waking up an hour earlier than normal. I set my alarm for five a.m. most days and woke up with a cup of coffee. I wrote my gratitudes and affirmations before the sun was up. I visualized the day before me and what I wanted to happen. I played cheesy music on Alexa when it was still dark outside and I was the only one in the kitchen. Sometimes I even danced.

Then I went down to our basement where we had some gym equipment. I created a playlist that both motivated and inspired me. Songs that spoke my truth. I blasted music and sang while I moved my body and lifted weights. After I was done, while getting ready for the day, I chose a positive YouTube video by someone like Tony Robbins, Larry Kendall, Oprah, Jim Rohn, or Les Brown (and many others) and listened to it while I did my hair and makeup.

Each morning was supercharged with gratitude and a positive mindset.

I wrote down my new goals. I stared at them. I willed them into existence. I took action, recognizing that I would find a path out of this dark forest. In fact, this was the time to find and climb a mountain as there was less traffic.

My friend Melanie Frank started a private Facebook page for realtors around the country focused on mindset, and we called each other, giddy on the phone. We had wanted to connect for the past few years, but both of us were so busy in our day-to-day professional life it never seemed to happen. Until now.

"Let's stream on Facebook Live," I offered.

"I was thinking the same!" she said. All my years of video production were now an asset and I could configure everything with Zoom (thank you AirPods and ring lights). Together, a group of us established an online community. It grew from a few hundred to over three thousand.

Coffee Talk, as we called it, became a big hit within our organization. Every Monday morning, Mel and I, along with Maria Vitale, hosted a FB Live for thousands around the country.

The messages poured in on chat, in DM, and on beautiful handwritten notes:

You ladies are helping me so much, thank you.

Thank you for talking about staying positive.

Thank you for starting my week with a positive mindset.

Thank you for sharing your personal journey.

I appreciate you so much.

Thank you, thank you.

We hosted a special session with Larry Kendall of *Ninja Selling* and Bob Burg, coauthor of *The Go-Giver*. I was nervous virtually meeting Bob (an amazing author and speaker), but he turned out to be one of the coolest people ever. The more I interacted with Larry and Bob, the more I felt my true purpose aligned with their work. I wanted to help others.

I enrolled in a program with Bob focused on being a "Go-Giver" certified speaker and coach. I used the COVID-19 downtime and studied on nights and weekends. Little did I know Bob would eventually become a mentor and friend.

COVID-19 accelerated many things. Our long-term dream of moving to a warm climate had new urgency. We wanted palm trees, the beach, and a new adventure. Our conversations became consumed by the idea of moving. I was ready to be a bigger contributor to an organization and wondered what that might look like workwise.

Then I heard through my professional network of a perfect job opportunity. In Florida.

It was everything I had prayed for.

RELENTLESS

After a few sleepless nights, I decided it was time to speak to my boss.

I owe some of my biggest gratitudes to Paul. He gave me a shot at my first management job, showed me how to read a P&L, and taught me the foundation of how to run a real estate company. The longer I worked for him, the more I saw the softer side. I admired how he would stop his day to take a call from his kids. He urged me to be strong but to lead with my heart.

He drove up at my request to meet. He arrived at the end of the day, sword in hand.

"Here is your sword," he handed me my "prize" for last year. I had placed first in recruiting within the company. A sword seemed fitting. It was my second one and he had it engraved.

I held it up. "This is awesome."

"It's a real sword. Don't cut yourself," he said. We laughed. "Shall we have our chat at The Corner?" The Corner was the bar/restaurant next door. So many of my life events played out at The Corner; it seemed like the movie set of my life.

We grabbed a table and ordered cocktails. I focused on my gratitude for him in that moment. It helped with the anxiety of the impending conversation. I waited until we had a few sips of our beverages.

"There is something we need to discuss."

"Are you leaving?" he asked. He was always direct.

"I think it's time."

He nodded. "Wow."

"I am not sure where I am going yet."

"Well, we have had a good run," he said in his deadpan humor. We smiled at each other. It had been a good run. A ton of growth personally and professionally.

"This is hard."

I explained we were ready as a family to relocate and we wanted to move out-of-state.

"I need your blessing."

"You are one of the hardest-working people I have ever met. You have taken every opportunity and ran with it. I am sorry to see you go but I want to see you happy."

Tears stung my eyes and gratitude welled up inside me. "I appreciate everything you have done for me. And I want you to know I won't leave until we have a plan for the office. Who knows if I will even find the right job?"

"How can I help you find the job you want?" he asked.

I was shocked at his generosity. It was more than I had hoped for.

"I heard there is an opportunity to work in Florida in a senior level position with the same brand."

"Do you want me to call the CEO? I know him well."

"That would be amazing."

About three weeks later, I interviewed for my dream job as the SVP for a large and prestigious company working alongside Budge, an icon in the real estate industry.

Paul always told me, "An opportunity is simply an invitation to sit at the table. You still have to prove your worth."

With some visualization, preparation, and a pocket of gratitude, I hoped and prayed.

Soon after, my two swords clanked and rattled in the car as we drove to Florida so I could start my new job.

"Are these swords even legal?" my husband asked. "Like if we get pulled over?"

"I have no idea. Let's hope we never find out."

A few months later, I wrote Paul a letter of gratitude.

It said something like:

You saw potential in me I did not know I had. Because you believed in me and gave me a chance, I grew stronger. Your opportunity was a gift that offered me what I needed to learn. Because of you, I have been able to provide for my family. You are the greatest teacher I have ever had. Thank you for making me better and for giving me a chance. I promise to make you proud.

Because of COVID-19, there was no going-away party or big announcement where I could hug everyone I had worked with for over ten years. It was bittersweet to drive away from our small town; from my people.

A few weeks later, a big, heavy package arrived. "What in god's name is this?" Ian asked.

I opened it. It was from Paul. It was a large bronze statue of a female Viking warrior, complete with sword. It was inscribed, "RELENTLESS."

I may (or may not have) teared when I opened it. I rubbed her little helmet head and found her a place of honor on my new shelf. We had fully embraced a new life complete with palm trees, a pool, and lanai.

But moving to Florida during the pandemic came at a price. My daughter, Amelia, still had to finish her senior year of high school. I agonized over the decision and told her about the job offer and what it might mean.

"You can move with us," I said months ago. "I know it's not ideal, but you could go to school in Florida. You are mostly online anyway."

"It's senior year. I am not going."

"I can say no to the job."

"I guess I can live with Dad," she said.

My gut was in a knot. I felt sick. I did not want to hurt her and it felt selfish. "If you want me to stay, I will pass on the job."

"I don't want you to leave, Mom, but you have worked so hard your entire life and it's such a big opportunity. You have to take it." I could not believe the maturity and love from my daughter. It moved me to tears.

"But will you go to college in Florida?" I asked. We had discussed it. At least that would offer a path for us to be together again. Eventually.

"I would like to."

"Do you want to live with your dad for the rest of the school year and then move to Florida? It's six months."

"I don't know," she said. "I think so."

A piece of my heart was broken at the thought of moving away without her. Was this the right thing to do? That old guilt jacket made a reappearance. I eyed it in the closet. I did not want to ever put it back on.

A few weeks later, we talked it out and set up a plan. We would see each other as much as possible. It was still COVID-19, and testing and quarantining after crossing state lines was still a thing.

"I'll be fine," she said.

We both knew this was the hardest thing we had ever faced.

"Are you sure?"

"You need to take this job, Mom," she reassured me.

"You know I love you more than anything in the world, right?"

"I know."

She gave me permission to pursue my dream, understanding it would be hard for her. Another big change. I was astonished at her maturity and strength.

My daughter is one of the best gifts of my life. She is one of the bravest people I know. Distance made our bond even stronger. Suddenly, all the silly teenage disagreements we used to have were a thing of the past. We missed each other. We appreciated each other. Even though we were separated by distance, we talked and texted all the time.

It was hard.

She was accepted into college and, after senior year, moved to Florida. We were together again. She is one of my greatest gratitudes.

One of the highlights of my life was a year later when Amelia handed me a "note of gratitude." She was prompted to write to "someone she was grateful for" in class.

This is what her note said:

Dear Mom,

Thanks for being my best friend. You do everything you can for me to be happy and always listen to my stories and complaints. You inspire me every day with how successful you are in work.

I aspire to be more like you every day. So glad for our close relationship and quality time.

Love,

Amelia

I have one word: heartmelt.

AFTER THE RAIN

COVID-19 was not as kind to others. So many people lost friends, family members, or suffered with their own debilitating health issues. People we knew passed away. It was horrible.

I still remember Mother's Day with my parents during deep COVID-19. We sat in the dining room of their house with the windows and doors open, hoping we would not infect each other.

I had never really appreciated how easy it was to gather with family.

I had never appreciated how easy it was to give someone a hug.

I had never appreciated things like in person meetings, travel, or concerts.

It is crazy how, when common things are suddenly taken away, you quickly appreciate them.

I decided it was time to start being the real me. To stop doubting myself. To be authentic. To grow.

In the podcast *We Can Do Hard Things*, Glennon Doyle talks openly about her struggles as a woman and mother. We all have them. She says, "This life is mine alone, so I have stopped asking people for directions to places they've never been."

For many, the pandemic was a magnifying glass. It helped us take pause and really look around. It taught us that nothing is guaranteed. Not holidays, prom, trips, or even our jobs or school. This perspective was life-altering.

The Habit of Grateful helps us consciously recognize blessings more fully. Otherwise, life is a merry-go-round; a blur of time. Stop and acknowledge your journey.

Where do you want to go next?

Gratitude Soup

It's a Saturday at the local grocery store and the aisles are jam-packed. Some shoppers are still wearing masks, but most are not. It is summer in Florida, and the pavement is already hot and sticky at ten a.m. The grocery store is a cool respite from the humidity and yet I cringe going from hot-hot to freezing once I am inside.

Weekends are a joy as I cling to some "me" time whenever I can find it. My new job is demanding but I love every moment of it. Growing a large organization and working with many talented individuals, it can easily take over my entire life, and I find myself more and more working nights and weekends to keep up with the hectic pace. I still have a problem of setting big goals and pushing myself to succeed.

I am here to buy ingredients for bean soup, or Gratitude Soup, as I like to call it. My great-grandmother, Amelia, was an incredible cook. She and my great-grandfather, Giuseppe Tuzzo, came to America from Northern Italy in the 1900s. My great-grandmother had eight siblings, and as one of the oldest, cared and cooked for her family.

Growing up, they watched my sister and I after school and in the summer.

"Kristina, your father, he go to worka today?" Nono asked, his pipe in one hand and his small glass of wine in the other.

"Yes, Nono," I answered, wondering why he could not ask more original questions. It was always the same three.

Nona always wore an apron and a dress, and with her shock of white hair and deep blue eyes, it was like she could stare right into your soul. "Stand straight. *Mangia*, Kristina. *Bellissima*."

They lived in a very modest three-room house behind a multi-family, but they had a garden, some grapes vines, and a wine cellar. Nono made his own wine, and some of my best memories were walking with Nona in the garden. She cut some lettuce, picked tomatoes from the vines and cucumbers, and tossed together the most beautiful salad I have ever had in my life, adding a shot of vinegar and some oil and salt. It was still warm from the sun when we ate it.

In the kitchen/living room, she loved to cook for all of us. I watched as she took dough and cut pasta and dried it in white boxes lined with paper under her bed. She simmered the most amazing brown stew and always seemed to have a pot of soup on the stove. She dried her own spices in the barn and made everything from scratch. I helped her make chicken stock and we later took the meat off the boiled chicken and ate it. She never let me throw out the fat. "The best part," she said. She never wasted anything.

Nono loved Corn Flakes and he added wine to them, then coffee and milk.

They did not have a couch, just some chairs. This bothered me because I did not like that they were poor. But they had cable, and Saturday mornings meant cartoons, which they let my sister and I watch. *He-Man. Tom & Jerry.* We lined up the chairs together and lay over them like a couch.

Nono told me he came to America to escape Italy. He was a policeman and had a horse, but he had to hide to not get hurt or worse. He came here to find a better life and a good job (his brother came first) and worked on the railroads until he had enough money to save for Nona, who then joined him. They had two children: my grandmother, Lena, and her sister, Enes.

My grandmother worked in a factory, as did my grandfather. Seeing her operate a huge machine on the stuffy fifth floor of the grimy manufacturing plant was eye-opening. It reeked of chemicals. The windows were covered with soot. The thought of my gram spending most of her adult life in such a gloomy place made me feel sad and angry at the same time.

I wish her life had been easier. But she was proud. I visited her at work. "My Kristina!" she called and came over to me. My grandmother showed me off to everyone on her floor saying things like, "Isn't she beautiful?" and, "She is going to college—so smart!" I was humbled and grateful for her love.

We always had so much family around it felt like I had a few sets of parents. My gram, aunt Enes, and Nono and Nona were the fibers of my childhood, and some days I tinkered in Nono's barn, or peeled paint chips off their house, or read through stacks of books my aunt bought me (we both shared a passion for reading). But my favorite was when I helped Nona cook and then did dishes in her extra wide, deep porcelain sink. She washed. I always dried.

Lunch was always the most special meal. A bowl of homemade soup and then something delicious. A pasta, a stew, small steaks, whipped potatoes, and then a big slice of Entenmann's fudge iced golden cake for dessert. They let me drink coffee.

The best dish Nona made was her bean soup. It was fundamentally different because the stock was made from beans, brown and thick. She then added whatever pasta she had and topped it with fresh Asiago cheese. Everything was always fresh. Nona walked to the market almost every day. When I went with her, she fussed and yelled at me for bad posture.

This brown soup was the nectar of my youth. I can't tell you how many times I slurped it down and asked for seconds. It was the most comforting thing in the world. She loved to watch us eat. It was love for her. In every bowl, on every plate. Her food was love.

I will never forget our last day. She was in her eighties by then and I was tall for my age. I was around eleven, and our family was at Nona and Nono's house. I think we were celebrating something—perhaps a birthday. We cleaned up together. Nona was at the sink and she handed me her red speckled dish towel. "Kristina, you dry."

"I can help. Go play," my mom said.

"No, Kristina. She dry," Nona said.

I was happy to be useful and tried to keep up with her. She washed the dishes and stacked them as I dried each one and put them away. We worked in silence, but it was the beautiful feeling of doing something together and feeling a strong sense of belonging. When she looked at me and smiled, it was so heartfelt that I felt absolute joy.

"Thank you, Kristina," she said and patted my hand.

"Your father, he go to worka today?" Nono asked, with his pipe.

Nona swore at him in Italian and we laughed.

The next day my mother started screaming. I heard her from my room and ran over to her. She was hysterical. "Nona died. She had a stroke."

"What?" I asked, not comprehending. "What?"

"She's gone, Kris."

This was my first experience with death. I was in shock. And then pain. All I could think about was that we had been doing dishes together just a few hours ago and now she was gone.

Many years later, when I became a young mother, I thought of Nona often. I tried to find the recipes of my childhood. I went twenty years without bean soup, as no one seemed to know how to make it. Years later, a family friend offered me the recipe. I cried when she wrote it in cursive on a piece of paper. It took a few tries, but I finally replicated it.

The bean soup recipe came to me at a time we struggled financially. Trips to the grocery store were tense. Each item on my list had a price next to it, so when I got to the register, I could afford my cart. Bean soup was the cheapest meal I could make: it was essentially beans and veggies and pasta. I could make a huge pot and it would last all week. I wondered if this is why Nona learned how to make it all those years ago on a farm in Italy, with so many siblings to feed.

To this day, bean soup is one of my all-time favorite meals. Now, when I go to the checkout line in Publix, I am grateful I have a full cart and am confident I can afford it all. When they ask me if I would like to donate to the food shelter, I say yes.

In that moment, I am so grateful for bean soup and a job. For a healthy family. For money to buy groceries. And butter. But also for my Nona, who showed me so much love, and for my Nono, who moved here to give us all a better life. When I think of them in their twenties, struggling to learn a new language, with only a few pairs of clothes and eating food from their garden, I am filled with such gratitude.

Did anyone in your family sacrifice to give you a better life? If so, can you thank them?

Grazie, Nona & Nona. ti amerò per sempre.

Kristina

RECIPE FOR GRATITUDE SOUP

Three cans red kidney beans, drained and rinsed

Two cans white cannellini beans, drained and rinsed

One large onion, chopped into quarters

Three large carrots, chopped into quarters

Two celery sticks, chopped in half

Four large potatoes, chopped into quarters

One tsp. salt

One box Ditalini pasta

Vegetable or chicken bouillon cubes to taste

Fill an extra-large soup pot (twelve quart minimum) with beans, onion, carrots, celery, potatoes, salt, and water. Boil four hours, covered. Pour and mash through a strainer into a large pan. Mash the solid ingredients until only pulp. Discard pulp.

Meanwhile, boil half a box Ditalini pasta until *al dente*. Strain.

Take soup broth (after it has been strained as described above) and reheat on stove to a simmer until thick. Add 1–2 bouillon cubes, salt, and grated cheese to taste. Add cooked and strained Ditalini pasta and let sit for fifteen minutes. Serve hot with extra Parmesan cheese on top and crusty bread on the side.

If you are a meat-eater, add a cube of pork salt to the stock instead of one teaspoon salt. I omit and it still tastes great!

Walk Your Way to Grateful

"If you are in a bad mood, go for a walk.
If you are still in a bad mood, go for
another walk."

—HIPPOCRATES

Another way to practice a habit of grateful is to take a
"Gratitude Walk." Cheryl Rickman, author of *The Flourish
Handbook* writes:

> Each morning I walk myself into a state of well-being
> and away from my worries. I walk myself into new ideas,
> creative solutions, and immense gratitude for what I have.
> With each step I feel empowered. But why is my gratitude
> walk so powerful? Fundamentally, it's the combination of
> two mood-boosting, stress-busting life-affirming tools
> being used together—walking and expressing gratitude
> simultaneously. (Rickman 2013)

Walking is not only a great form of exercise, but therapeutic. It has many health benefits, such as increased endorphins that decrease stress, increased heart health, circulation in the body, and decreased blood pressure. Walking also frees our mind from technology and distraction and can make it easier to tap into your inner stream of consciousness. Couple this activity with a focus on gratitude, and you create an easy way to cultivate your habit of grateful.

I try to incorporate gratitude walks as much as I can. As soon as my feet hit the ground, I remind myself how lucky I am that I can walk without pain. I see a little lizard cross my path and another bounds up a tree. I am grateful for palm trees and a lush, tropical landscape. I spent most of my life in New England surrounded by barns and cows. Forests.

Here in Florida, the sun beams twenty-four seven and everything just feels happy. I waved to a neighbor. Down the street, I crossed paths with another neighbor. They had their dog hooked up to a contraption where his rear legs used to be, allowing him to walk even though he only has two front legs. He panted and looked happy with the wheels whizzing behind him. This, too, made me feel joyous and grateful for compassionate people who nurtured this injured dog. How beautiful.

The goal of the gratitude walk is to drink in the things you see around you and observe with your senses. Notice how this feels. Notice each breath, each blade of grass, each step forward.

In an article for the *Huffington Post*, Cheryl Rickman offers tips on how to take a gratitude walk (Rickman 2013):

- Walk alone if possible (you can't think if you're chatting to a friend).

- Find a peaceful location to walk in with minimal distractions or people around. The more literal space you have, the more breathing space you'll have and the more freeing the walk will be.

- Take a notepad and pen so you can jot down a list of ten things you are completely grateful for. Feel that gratitude, then walk on. Also jot down any ideas about projects to pursue or actions to take.

- Take a deep breath in for five and out for five and notice your surroundings. Keep your head up as you walk. Look around you, breathe it all in, and let those creative thoughts flow.

- Find time to walk regularly. Just fifteen minutes per day or even every other day will have a positive impact on your life.

You can embrace the principle of a gratitude walk with a quick jaunt around your neighborhood. For others, walking can also mean immersing oneself into Mother Nature and getting away from developed areas. Consider taking time to find a special nature preserve or trail to hike.

In the memoir *Wild: From Lost to Found on the Pacific Crest Trail* (2012), Cheryl Strayed chronicles her 1,100-mile journey on the Pacific Crest Trail after personal struggles and it is the story of self-discovery and triumph. She backpacks alone through deep wilderness that challenges her body and mind.

And yet it is not only her journey, and discovery of deep strength, but the wild surroundings that shape her. Strayed writes:

> That perhaps being amidst the undesecrated beauty of the wilderness meant I too could be undesecrated, regardless of the regrettable things I'd done to others or myself or the regrettable things that had been done to me. Of all the things I'd been skeptical about, I didn't feel skeptical about this: the wilderness had a clarity that included me. (Rickman 2013)

While extreme, her bravery is documented by transformative writing and haunting self-reflection. Nature teaches many lessons and perhaps there is ancient healing magic for all of us inside caves and waterfalls. Perhaps nature can baptize us with her cleansing waters. Whispers of tree branches or the symphony of a summer night. Perhaps nature can offer healing not backed by science and computers. The simple act of walking in nature (or the wild) is perhaps one of the easiest ways to reflect on your mindset and sweep out those cobwebs of negativity.

Gratitude to Nature Mantra

You are a child of the universe.
You belong here.
You were made strong for this world; of water and air and everything that is good and right.

Feel your heartbeat.
Listen how it says, proudly,
LIVE.

Louie Schwartzberg is an expert on gratitude and uses cinematography to illuminate the miracles of nature. Do yourself the favor of googling him and watch some of his incredible videos. He uses timelapse and micro-lenses to capture the sheer brilliance of nature all around us (Schwartzberg 2022). He says, "I hope my films inspire and open people's hearts. Beauty is nature's tool for survival—we protect what we love. That is the shift in consciousness we need to sustain and celebrate life" (2022).

Schwartzberg has a whole series on gratitude and his images of nature evoke awe and wonder. His latest project is entitled "Gratitude Revealed" and is simply stunning. His lens (and dare I say it's rose-colored) is like a microscope as he unveils the beauty of the ordinary right under us. If you can't go for a walk, you can spend some time watching his work at MovingArt.com for inspiration.

Deepak Chopra is a spiritual guru and author of over ninety books translated into over forty-three languages, including numerous *New York Times* bestsellers. On his website, Chopra.com, he recommends a gratitude walk, particularly when stressed.

> As you walk, […] breathe, pause, and be grateful for the air that is filling your lungs and making your life possible. Pay attention to your senses—everything you're seeing, hearing, feeling, smelling, and maybe even tasting—and see how many things you can find to feel grateful for. This is a powerful way to shift your mood and open to the flow of abundance that always surrounds you. (The Editors at Chopra 2012)

Let's try it! Set aside some time and commit to a gratitude walk.

TAKE A GRATITUDE WALK

- Twenty to forty-five minutes.

- Get rid of distractions like your phone or music.

- Get outside and walk in nature.

- Let the sounds of nature fill your ears.

- Where is the sun in the sky? What color is the sky?

- Watch the sky for clouds or birds; what do you see?

- Look for flowers, trees, and plants.

- What do you notice that is special? What is beautiful?

- Take some time to feel grateful for the miracles of nature, for the sky, the earth, for water, and for sun.

- Can you thank Mother Nature for these gifts?

- What are you most grateful for in this moment?

ONE MORE REMINDER

I was speaking at a realtor event in Connecticut about gratitude. Afterward, a woman came up to me.

"My husband passed away not long ago. He was diagnosed with terminal cancer, and we were told he only had a few months to live. We did not have much, but we had gratitude. So each day we wrote on sticky notes things we were grateful for. We lined the hallway with words on yellow notes. Things like the stars, a sunrise, the flowers in our garden. Butterflies. Things that didn't cost anything. We made it a point to get outside together. To take in nature each day. And eventually when the hallway was lined with stickies, we felt so rich. Wealthy with all these free gifts."

I squeezed her hand.

Let us never forget to be grateful for the miracles of this Earth. Of water and air, day and night. For a blue sky, stars, and creatures large and small. The sound of waves, the crackle of fire, the magic of a butterfly, and the exquisite detail of a tulip.

Let us not take for granted the beauty.

Mary

"Gratitude is the memory of the heart."

—JEAN-BAPTISTE MASSIEU

Long before my friend Mary took us to the lake that summer when my world was crashing down, we enjoyed many weekends together. Before I went into real estate, I had a gig as a wedding videographer to supplement my income. I was introduced to Mary and she started to give out my business card. Mary was a teacher and a wedding photographer on the weekends.

We instantly clicked.

I'll never forget one Saturday morning, I stood outside a beautiful stone church in Bristol, my feet already pinching from new flats. I had been to the bride's house and had videotaped her and her friends as they had makeup and hair done and sipped champagne. Mary was the photographer, and she set up some creative shots with the bride's dress and flowers. Her calm energy and big smile put everyone at ease.

The bride's limo pulled up to the church and Mary's car did too. Her daughter, Alyssa (not much younger than me), trailed along and they both had handfuls of gear and cameras. They hustled and followed the bride's every move; cameras clicking in unison.

Mary and I stood side by side.

"You are doing such a great job," she said to me.

"Trying," I said and laughed.

"It is so great to be here with you. I am so thankful," her words were sincere and from the heart. "You are very special to me."

It made me uncomfortable. I was not used to open praise. "Me too," I said, feeling a little weird in a good way.

We spent many a Saturday from sunup to sundown shooting weddings together. She was a perfectionist. I was paranoid about two things: video tape and batteries. Mary effortlessly spoke to the bride and groom and directed them to pose, to kiss, and to look over their shoulders. Weddings by nature are stressful, but Mary put everyone at ease. She made them smile and laugh. She was magnetic.

Over the years we shared our creative passions. I painted and wrote and she encouraged it. She was on a spiritual quest of sorts and wrestled with the passing of her mother and father. We exchanged books and letters. We enjoyed long conversations on the phone talking about life and stress and family and friends.

When I had my second son, she dropped off premade meals with sticky notes on them. Lasagna: *Heat to 350 degrees.* A big bowl of salad, complete with dressing and croutons: *Enjoy.* She also brought designer hand-me-down clothes (which I appreciated), or something thoughtful like a small necklace or special card. But the best gifts were her humor, her smile, and a zest for living in a positive mindset. Each year she wrote a holiday letter so funny that it brought me to tears.

Her photographs always captured something deeper than just a picture. She possessed a raw talent for capturing the essence of that person. Mary saw the light in others, in film and in life.

Our friendship blossomed over many years. She was unwavering in her encouragement and I can't even count the number of times I called her, my heart bursting with disappointment or burning with some type of hurt. Her friendship was a life raft.

She called me her "special Kristine." Each time I spoke with her, I felt grateful and honored we were friends; that she believed in me.

In an article called "Why Gratitude Is Good," Robert Emmons says:

> Grateful people have a higher sense of self-worth. Once you start to recognize the contributions that other people have made to your life—once you realize that other people have seen the value in you—you can transform the way you see yourself. (Emmons 2010)

Another friend, Maria Vitale, recently told me, "If you could only see yourself the way others see you, you would be pretty impressed." There is a truth to that for each one of us. How do your friends perceive you? Are you as kind to yourself?

It took time for me to feel worthy; especially in the beginning. I thought, *Why would she want to be my friend? I am a nobody.* I had a lot of self-doubt. She had a nicer house, more material things, and was very successful. I was a young struggling mom who could barely afford groceries. I was a college dropout. I lived in a half-finished, run-down farmhouse that was always a mess.

What I learned many years later is the biggest gift you have to offer to the world is yourself. You are enough. If I could write this across this sky in huge letters I would:

YOU ARE ENOUGH.

YOU ARE A GIFT.

As Bob Burg states in *The Go-Giver: A Little Story About a Powerful Business Idea*, "The most valuable gift you have to offer is yourself" (Burg and Mann 2015). It took me a long time to embrace this. My failures did not have to be embarrassments. My failures made me stronger. Most very successful people have failed at something. Or many things. Some very public. People like Steve Jobs, Elon Musk, and Oprah have all talked publicly about their failures but they refused to let their past define them.

Looking back, Mary was a big part of my journey. She saw something special in me that I did not.

"You are so talented."

Her words pinged off me like sleet hitting a roof. "No. No," I said. "*I am not.*" I felt such deep shame and embarrassment.

She looked me in the eyes and told me again, "You are strong. You are kind. And you are beautiful, inside and out."

The words softened upon impact. Eventually when I took down my walls of shame, she got through to my heart. Never underestimate how kindness can impact others and how you can change someone's life with something as simple as your words.

Mary and I wrote letters to each other. We shared gratitudes and we sent poems back and forth. She was a cherished friend and mentor. Ten years went by in a flash. Triston, who had been a chubby baby we once brought to a field of daffodils to photograph, became a tall and confident young man who graduated from middle school. Then high school.

After Ian and I got engaged, we decided to have a very small intimate ceremony and dinner. Just with the kids, parents, and close family. I was low-key about the details as we were not planning anything extravagant. I was going to go look for a wedding dress alone until Mary offered to help me shop. We walked in and out of bridal shops. Nothing looked right. "I don't think I want to wear white," I said.

"Then don't. It's your wedding."

This time, I would wear a dress befitting the woman I had become. We entered another bridal store. "She doesn't want white," Mary offered to the saleswoman who guessed my size. "And she is expecting, so we need some give." Mary winked.

Ian and I had found out we had a baby on the way. We were a little nervous, but so excited.

"I did white last time. It's time for a new me. Any 'in' colors for the second time around?" I joked.

"Just white," The salesclerk said.

Mary and I looked through racks and racks of dresses. Then I saw it: a soft teal blue made of long, flowing satin with an off-the-shoulder top. She helped me try it on.

It was perfect. It was me.

"Wow," she said. We stared at each other and smiled the way good friends do.

"This is the one," I said.

One fine day in autumn, Ian and I walked through grass dotted with leaves before our wedding ceremony. Mary followed us around with her camera and clicked away.

"This is what true love looks like," she said. "You are both so happy, you radiate." Mary hugged me and I remembered long ago how lonely I had been and how she urged me on and leant me strength.

Summers came and went.

A few years later, Mary had a medical emergency. I went to the hospital, not sure what to expect. Her husband was there with her, looking tired in a big brown chair. She was propped up with pillows, her body kind of flat.

She could not really talk but she started with a soft coo. "Oooo," she said with recognition. "K-K-K-Kristine," she said, barely able to pronounce my name.

It was her heart talking to mine, and I held back my tears. "Hello, beautiful friend."

"Oooo," she said. She tried to talk but could not find the words.

I nodded and smiled at her. I held her hand.

She would never fully recover.

A few months later, her daughter, Alyssa, came to see me. She has her mother's eyes. We sat close to each other. I put my hand on her arm. Her young children, aged three and one, were balls of energy and ran around us.

"She always wanted grandkids," I said and smiled through my tears. "We always talked about it. She is so proud of you and loves them so much."

"She is dying," Alyssa said. "You should go see her."

I nodded. Our tears fell like hot lava, seeping into my shirt and pants.

The drive to the hospital was long. This time, she was not awake. Her husband hugged me. His eyes were bloodshot.

"It is so good you came. She would want you to be here."

"How are you holding up?" I asked.

He shrugged. "This is hard," he wiped his eyes. "Would you like to say goodbye?"

"Yes. Thank you."

"The doctors said she can hear you, even if she doesn't open her eyes. I will leave you two alone." He patted my shoulder and left the room.

This time I did not try to be brave. I cried, letting tears flow as my mind drifted in and out of so many memories. I sat next to her. Mary looked so tiny in the hospital bed, the white sheets swallowing her. I put my hand on her arm and leaned in closer.

I told her:

"I know I have to say goodbye, but I don't know how. All the memories, all those happy moments. How you could make me laugh so hard that my stomach hurt. And the hard times, how you were right there by my side.

I don't think I would have gotten through the divorce without you, Mary. You lent me courage. You believed in me when I could not even look in the mirror; you always told me 'you can do it.'"

And I did.

Because of you, Mary.

"I can't even imagine a world without you in it; that it could even happen. I don't want to lose you, Mary. I don't want to say goodbye, my beautiful friend."

Sunshine illuminated the room. It poured in and bathed us in bright white light.

"But I know that it is your time to go. And I want you to walk into that big white light and into heaven. Be in peace in that special, beautiful place that is the other side.

And know I will keep you in my heart forever. Every smile, each act of kindness. You will forever be inside me."

I saw her husband at the door.

I whispered to her, "You are strong. You are smart. You are kind. And you are beautiful, inside and out. Goodbye my friend, I love you."

It was the last time I saw her.

Habit #4—Commit

"The moment you commit and quit holding back, all sorts of unforeseen incidents, meetings, and material assistance will rise up to help you. The simple act of commitment is a powerful magnet for help."

—NAPOLEON HILL

- **Habit #4—Commit**

  o Vitamin G: take your gratitude pill every day

  o Make gratitude a morning/evening habit

  o Track your progress

  o Sign a gratitude contract

The last Habit of Grateful is the hardest but the most rewarding. It requires an absolute commitment to living a life filled with an "attitude of gratitude." This widely known phrase represents the desire to express thankfulness and appreciation for every part of your life. Having an attitude of gratitude means you live in a mindset of abundance, rather than scarcity.

If you commit to daily habits of gratitude, you will see results. But first this requires an honest conversation with yourself. What benefits might gratitude give you?

Are you seeking a way to feel better and attain more happiness?

Do you want to form stronger relationships with others?

Would you like to live in a positive mindset of abundance?

If these are some of the things you want to work on, there is bad news and good news. The bad news is you are the only one who can make these changes and, therefore, a commitment. The good news is you are the only one who can make these changes and a commitment.

Brené Brown, PhD, is a research professor at the University of Houston Graduate College of Social Work. She has spent the past two decades studying vulnerability, courage, worthiness, and shame. She is the author of *The Gifts of Imperfection*, *Daring Greatly*, *Rising Strong*, *Braving the Wilderness*, and *Dare to Lead*.

Brown says that practicing gratitude is the key to joy. "Without exception, every person I interviewed who described living a joyful life actively practiced gratitude and attributed joyfulness to that practice" (Brown 2019).

When we talk about the benefits of gratitude, commitment is crucial. A habit is behavior you replicate daily and with intention. But first you must commit to the process by believing in yourself.

Can you sign a contract with yourself to commit to the Habit of Grateful?

Take out a piece of paper. At the top, write:

"MY CONTRACT—THE HABIT OF GRATEFUL"

I, (Insert your name), commit to a daily habit of gratitude to improve not only my happiness, but the lives of all those around me. I will start each day with gratitude and look for opportunities to tell others how much I appreciate them. I understand gratitude is the key to a healthier and happier life of abundance, and I fully accept all the gifts that result from a life of gratitude.

I sign my name to this formula and commit it to memory with full FAITH that it will gradually influence my THOUGHTS and ACTIONS.

(Sign and date your name)

Keep a picture of this in your phone or hang it somewhere you will see it. You can repeat this pledge to yourself daily if you would like to have even bigger results. Be sure to give it attention and remember to always honor your commitment to yourself.

And congratulations for taking this step!

HEALTH BENEFITS

"Gratitude is a vaccine, an antitoxin, and an antiseptic."

—JOHN HENRY JOWETT (1863–1923)

Making a conscious effort every day to focus on gratitude is like taking a vitamin for your spiritual and mental health: the habits of grateful are your vitamins. Take them every single day to stay healthy and happy. They are "Vitamin G."

There is a powerful connection between our body and mind. When we feel anxious or overwhelmed, our nervous system sounds off an alarm and goes into a high state of alert. Stress hormones like cortisol flood the body. Over time, constant flooding can produce physical symptoms like high blood pressure, inflammation, and others. The wave of calm washing over us when we concentrate on gratitude transmits a message to our bodies that "all is well," quieting these stress responses. "Feelings of gratitude trigger the parasympathetic, or calming, branch of the nervous system," says Emmons (2016).

There are countless studies demonstrating the health benefits of gratitude. Almost all of them require commitment. You must make gratitude part of your daily routine to fully reap the benefits.

Results from the GGSC's Thnx4 project found that participants who kept an online gratitude journal for two weeks reported better physical health, including fewer headaches, less stomach pain, clearer skin, and reduced congestion. (Simon-Thomas 2012)

People with heart failure (Mills et al. 2015) and chronic pain who are more grateful report sleeping better, despite their condition, than less grateful patients (Ng and Wong 2013). In a study of 401 people, 40 percent of whom had clinically impaired sleep, more grateful people reported falling asleep more quickly, sleeping longer, having better sleep quality, and staying awake more easily during the day. This study also found evidence that more grateful people sleep better because they have fewer negative thoughts and more positive ones at bedtime (Wood 2019).

If you are a skeptic, that's okay. Skeptics question everything but are willing to look at data. If you are totally closed off from believing in gratitude, my recommendation is to test it out for thirty days. Think of it as a science experiment. If after thirty days you do not feel any benefits, then perhaps gratitude is more of a "once in a while" type of thing for you.

Give it a shot!

GRATITUDE TRACKER

If you use a calendar, make a reoccurring invitation on it that says "SSG": Show Some Gratitude. Denote on your calendar when you have consciously practiced your gratitude.

Grab a journal, spiral notebook, etc. Each day, write the date and jot down what you are grateful for. Try to do this every single day.

Put up a sticky note in your bathroom that says "Gratitude." Put a dot or star on it each day you practice your gratitude. When it is full, replace it with a new sticky.

Or just keep track of it to your best ability. Find your own ritual and morning routine. Use what works best for you.

Public service announcement: Keep your Vitamin G in your back pocket and dose heavily.

Daisy the Wonder Dog

"Dogs have a way of finding the people who need them and filling an emptiness we didn't ever know we had."

—THOM JONES

After many years, Frankie was still with us but in her senior years. Part deaf, half blind, she loved being alone in a quiet corner curled up on her poofy dog bed. Through it all, she had endured quite the journey. We knew it was time to look for another dog to be a companion to Frankie and our family.

We got on various breeder's lists and patiently searched. What kind of dog did we want? I knew we wanted a dog we could connect with that would bring us joy. In return, we would provide a wonderful and loving home. We thought about buying a dog and looked online.

No matter how much we searched, we could not seem to find the right dog.

Then, one Sunday on a whim, we decided to go to the Humane Society. Liam and I looked online and saw several cute dogs.

"Let's just look," I said to my husband.

"Okay," he said. "Worth a shot."

Visiting an animal shelter felt sad. We were overwhelmed by the number of dogs in need as Ian, Liam, and I arrived. Our volunteer was wonderful and spent time with us asking what type of dog we wanted to adopt. She screened us to make sure we could commit the time it takes to care for and settle in a new pet.

"Let's have you meet a few of our special folks," she said. "I'll bring you into a room where you can hang out and we will introduce you to a few dogs."

"Sounds great," we said as we walked down the hall of the beautiful new Humane Society. There were dozens of volunteers and various people with dogs. In one glass-windowed room, the cutest small brown dog cowered in the corner. A family with small children fawned over it. I stopped. She looked up at me with hopeless brown eyes.

"That dog is adorable. Is she available?"

"Wow, Mom, she is so cute," Liam said.

"Sorry, but that dog is already adopted. She is just spending time with her new family before she heads home."

"Lucky them," I smiled.

As we rounded the corner, I could not help but think of that small brown dog. Something in my heart stirred.

In our little room with a glass window, our volunteer brought in a large Shepherd mix. Liam and I backed up and Ian reached out to pet the big guy.

"He's cute," my husband said.

"He's big."

I felt a bit guilty, but ultimately a big dog made me feel uneasy.

"It has to be the right fit for all three of you," our volunteer said, watching Liam shake his head *no*.

We met a few more dogs but none felt right.

The volunteer took us into the back of the shelter and we walked down a long row of dogs, all homeless, just waiting for someone to adopt them. I felt guilty.

"Again, it has to be the right fit. We get dogs in need almost daily, so we can keep in touch," she said. "We are a no-kill shelter."

I had not thought about this. "Are there really still shelters that do that?"

"Yes, many," she said.

I looked at my husband. He shook his head.

"That is horrible. We would like to make a donation," I said. "Thank you for all you are doing to help these dogs. I really appreciate you." Not only was this woman simply amazing and cared about the dogs, but she was volunteering her time to make a difference.

"We can come back another time. I think we really want to stick to a small dog. It's just what we are used to and comfortable with."

As we were gathering our things, the volunteer came back into the room. "That brown dog you saw? Turns out that family is not adopting her. So, if you want to meet her, she is available."

"What?" Liam cheered. "Really?"

"But I have to warn you. She has heartworm. She will need medical treatment and there are some risks. She also has kennel cough and tapeworm. And a broken tail. In fact, the other family decided it was just too much. Visits with the vet and strict protocol so her heart rate does not go up for the first few months—is that something you would consider?"

I looked at Ian. He was, after all, the dog whisperer of our family.

"I think so," he said.

"Okay, well, let's have you meet her."

The minute Daisy came into the room, we fell in love with her. Her fur was a tangled mess and it was chopped off in places. She looked scared. She was tiny—about nine pounds. Half Chihuahua, half long-haired Dachshund. Our volunteer said, "She came in from an owner surrender in Houston. We got a truckload of dogs from Texas."

Ian rubbed behind her ears and she closed her eyes in appreciation.

I bent down to pet her. She stared up at me and melted my heart.

"Welcome to our family," Liam said.

The minute Daisy got home, she explored her new home and met Frankie. We bathed her in the sink and got all kinds of gross things out of her fur. She shook with fear. I wrapped her up in a blanket and we sat on the couch.

In time, she got comfortable. In fact, we still sing songs to her and she rolls over and points her paws to the air like she is giving thanks. I am so grateful we found her and for the wonderful volunteers at the Humane Society who saved her life and the lives of so many other animals.

My friend Lisa also adopted a rescue dog. She told me, "Bandit came into my life at a time when I needed a soulmate. My husband and I divorced. I started a new life. Bandit and I began exploring on the weekends. Work took me on road trips around Colorado and Bandit would join me. He'd sleep under a conference table snoring. After many years together, so much travel, and so much love, Bandit fell ill. He would not make it."

Lisa said, "Thanksgiving turned into a long and sleepless night. At three a.m., Bandit collapsed on the kitchen floor. I sat beside him, petting him for two hours. It was time. I carried him to the car for his last ride wrapped in a blanket. The vet was waiting and welcomed me into his office despite COVID-19. We stayed with him until he fell into his forever sleep. And when he crossed the rainbow bridge, we walked out with an enormous piece of us missing. Hearts aching."

Animals can teach us about life and love. They can simplify things and accept care and food unconditionally. They are loyal and love without demanding anything in return.

My friend Tracy is dedicated to helping animals. She said, "Every morning when I say my gratitudes, they always include our furry kids. Not a day goes by that I do not appreciate their unconditional love, their emotional support, and continued efforts to bring us joy."

Fur babies bring such joy and have deep gratitude for humans who give them a safe home. This bond is like nothing else.

Lisa said, "I thought I was rescuing Bandit, but in fact, he rescued me. I am grateful to him."

Have you felt gratitude for an animal? If so, how did that impact your life?

The Eye of the Storm

I have too many scars to count. My body is a road map of surgeries and survival, but these battle scars or rites of passage are reminders of things I am grateful for: a life well-lived.

Even now.

It was a burning hot day and I found myself with a group of parents around the community pool. Liam just turned eleven and we hosted a birthday party. I struck up a conversation with a petite brunette mom. She had on a wide-brimmed hat and her face was pasty with sunscreen.

"Hi, I'm Emily," she said.

As we got to know each other, I discovered she was a dermatologist and runs a large practice; hence the sunscreen and big hat.

"Oh wow, I am so happy to have met you. Since moving here, I am overdue for my annual skin checkup. It's hard to find new doctors."

"Don't let too much time go by. It's so important to get checked," she said. "At our practice, we pride ourselves on catching skin cancer as early as possible. You can go to any one of our offices, they are close by. We would love to have you as a patient."

"Wow. Thanks for the reminder. Good to know." I immediately liked her. She was cool.

We both watched kids sloshing around in the pool. Then, somehow, we started talking about gratitude (shocker) and Emily was suddenly energized. "I practice gratitude!" she said.

"It's amazing how many of us do—there is like a whole army of underground gratitude enthusiasts," I said. "Tell me more."

She said, "Since the kids were little, every night, at dinner. We go around the table and each one of us says one thing we are grateful for. Not only is it a chance for us as a family to catch up with each other, but it has helped us to focus on the positive things that happen each day. When you ask kids about their day, they struggle to really elaborate. But by asking them to share one thing from their day they are grateful for, we illuminate one thing from that day and share."

"How awesome!"

"Yes, it is something we all look forward to every night."

A few months later, I scheduled my routine skin cancer check and annual dermatology appointment at one of Emily's offices. I have light skin and blue eyes, and a galaxy of moles, and have been consistent with getting cancer scans. Since our move a few years ago, I was overdue.

I met the doctor and she spent some time talking with me and looking for anything suspicious. She stopped at my face. "That will need to be biopsied," she said, looking at a raised skin-colored mole on my cheek. "How long have you had this growth?"

"That? I have had that forever. In Connecticut, my dermatologist said it was nothing to be concerned about."

She held up a magnifying gadget with a blue light. "It needs to be biopsied."

"What does that mean?"

"I need to take a small piece of it out now so we can send it out to be studied. I think it is highly likely it's cancerous."

My face? I thought. I was at the age where I was now getting regular facials, micro-needling, and investing small fortunes in the latest antiaging lotions and serums.

"But I have a business meeting tonight and I am traveling. I am going to New York in a few days."

"You will be fine. We will put a Band-Aid on it."

"But my birthday is next week. We are going to the beach."

"Kristine, this *needs to be biopsied.*"

The fixer in me did not see any other options. "Can I come back in a month?"

"Not a good idea."

"Okay then." The doctor and assistant went over the procedure and aftercare instructions. First, I had to be numbed, which meant some needles in my cheek. I winced. A few minutes later, when I was numb, the doctor took a biopsy. "I am going to cauterize this. It may smell bad," she said.

It did.

Then I got my Band-Aid, which was the size of a half dollar.

"We will have the results in about a week. If it is cancerous, we have some options. Mohs surgery is usually the best. We also have some new creams and other things, but the safest thing is to have it removed."

When I got the call a week later, I had just landed at the new La Guardia airport for a work trip. It was shiny and sleek with lounge sitting areas, bright abstract lights, and polished wood. I found a chair and took the call.

"Hi Kristine. Your tests came back as basal skin cell carcinoma, and we will have to remove the growth. The doctor is recommending Mohs surgery. We can help you schedule with the facial plastic surgeon after so he can close the wound if you would like."

The words shocked me.

I had spent the last week with a Band-Aid on my face and tried my best to not be vain. I never realized how much I was on

Zooms and in meetings. Everyone looked at my Band-Aid and I politely offered up a joke. Now I would need to have a surgery and would have a pretty good-sized scar on my left cheek. Four inches long. I was scared. What would I look like afterward? What if it was even deeper than they thought? What if the cells were more cancerous than they anticipated?

Because BCCs grow slowly, most are curable and cause minimal damage when caught and treated early. So, of course, I started googling "images Mohs surgery face" (which I don't recommend). I accelerated into a full-blown panic. Would I be disfigured? Would my husband still find me attractive?

SkinCancer.org states: Basal cell carcinoma (BCC) is the most common form of skin cancer and the most frequently occurring form of all cancers. In the US alone, an estimated 3.6 million cases are diagnosed each year. BCCs arise from abnormal, uncontrolled growth of basal cells (Karen 2022). I was lucky the doctor properly diagnosed and found it early. Left untreated on the face, it could lead to cancer spreading.

Each time I started to freak out, I practiced gratitude by reminding myself of all I am grateful for, taking a gratitude walk, journaling, and reminding myself not to be a victim. Even for me, this took some redirecting of negative energy. It is not always easy to stay positive. In fact, a tiny voice inside you will point you to the "dark" side whenever you suffer disappointments or challenges. That is normal. Acknowledge that voice and let it know you appreciate the concern, but now you will be changing the channel to the positive. You have a choir inside you. They are called positive thoughts. Cue them to start singing. Then start dancing. Even if it's a slow dance, that's okay. You can work your way up to a fist pump.

I scheduled the surgery for about a month out. I moved up a professional photo shoot, not knowing how bad my face would look after the procedure.

The day of the surgery, I arrived at the dermatologist and was prepped for the procedure. After they numbed my right cheek (probably the worst part), the doctor went to work. I felt pressure and she talked me through it. Then cauterization. Then a big bandage.

"Give us about thirty minutes so we can examine the tissue and we will let you know if we have it all. You did great!"

I was escorted to a lounge waiting area. All of us patients waited to hear if the surgeon had cut out enough tissue. An older woman sat her leg in the air with a big gauze pad on her ankle. Another had her arm bandaged. A man in his fifties had a huge Band-Aid on the bridge of his nose that almost covered his eye.

"Join the party," one said. They were laughing and talking. I tried to smile, but my cheek wouldn't let me. I still felt a little woozy.

"I'm smiling inside," I said, pointing to my cheek.

They laughed.

In that moment, I started to feel a little sorry for myself. So, I consciously focused on everything I was grateful for. My husband.

My children. My dogs. Sunlight. Health insurance. My health. My parents. My friends. An upcoming trip. A savings account.

The doctor's assistant called me back into the surgery room; turned out they needed to go deeper. Thankfully, it was the last pass. They eventually bandaged me and I drove across town to a plastic surgeon who expertly stitched me up.

When he was done, he showed me a picture of the hole in the side of my face (prior to stitching it up). I almost passed out. It was a large crater. Then he handed me a mirror and showed me the caterpillar-like stitch across my cheek: easily four inches long. It was huge. "Ugh," I said.

"It looks great," my husband said, squeezing my hand.

We both knew it did not look great.

Perhaps my optimism was finally wearing off on him.

I studied the new addition of a fresh scar to my face. Without makeup on, there were also age spots and wrinkles. "Yikes," I said out loud.

"You are still beautiful," he said.

In the mirror, I found my own eyes. They sparkled back at me and I saw inside myself a quiet but determined kindness. I knew I would be okay.

"Thank you, Dr. Bhanot," I said. "I appreciate you!"

He smiled back.

That weekend was Labor Day. We had plans to take Liam to Disney World. "No Disney for you. You need to rest," the surgeon said. "It is important to stay out of the sun and not get your heart rate up. We don't want extra blood flow to the face."

We drove home in silence and I tried to stay positive. *Couch surfing would be good for me*, I told myself. Some "me time."

We were invited to picnics and gatherings, but I stayed home. I tried to not have a pity party for myself, but it was hard. I focused on the fact that I had taken proactive measures for my health. I thought of others I knew who battled cancer or, god forbid, passed away from it. I was lucky.

Bored on the couch, I decided to start posting some of the professional headshots I had just gotten back. The photographer had done amazing work and really captured me. So many people liked my photos on FB and Instagram. I kept seeing the comment *beautiful*.

It felt wrong.

Here I was on the couch with a face like Edward Scissorhands or Frankenstein's monster, yet on social media, I had these airbrushed photos of me in a light blue suit, just beaming. So happy. Grateful.

In reality, I was in sweatpants eating potato chips feeling sorry for myself.

I wanted to come clean.

So, I made a Reels video on Instagram showing my professional photo shoot and then the selfies I had been taking since my surgery.

"Are you really posting that?" my husband asked. He hates public displays. "Isn't it too personal?"

I saved it as a draft.

But the next day, I got even more comments on my new headshots.

I took my Reels and wrote "Grateful for this" and shared my story. I started with pictures of the professional headshots and then showed my newly scarred face with the stitches in and stitches out.

And I posted it for the world to see.

Gulp.

I was astounded by the love and support. So many people shared their own stories of similar skin cancer removals. Friends and colleagues from around the country texted and called.

They said:

You got this.
Still beautiful.
Thank you for sharing.

You are brave.

Because of you, I am getting my skin checked.

You are so strong.

You are an inspiration.

Thank you.

So proud of you.

Scars are hot.

And then my favorite: *I am grateful for you.*

THE MIRROR IN YOUR POCKET

There is one certain thing: life will always have disappointments. Loss. Failure. Pain. The road in front of you will continue to twist and turn. Change is inevitable.

Or, as my dad says, "Shit happens."

But in those moments of darkness and stress, remember that gratitude is a mirror in your pocket. It is your superpower. All you need to do is look into the mirror to reflect upon all that you are grateful for.

It will be hard sometimes to believe there is an easy solution; that you yourself have the power to change the way you feel. You will doubt the power of gratitude, you will eye-roll, and you might even give up.

There is a saying: "The moment you're ready to quit is usually the moment right before a miracle happens. Don't give up."
—Unknown.

Don't give up before gratitude has a chance to work its magic.

If you stick with a Habit of Grateful and practice gratitude each day, you will see benefits. You may also find yourself making better life choices, like going to bed earlier, eating well, and other healthy decisions. That is because in time, studies show gratitude may help us resist the appeal of instant gratification.

Our worst habits are rooted in impulsive decisions. Dr. David DeSteno, an expert in gratitude, is an author and professor of psychology at Northeastern University and Director of the Social Emotions Group. DeSteno found in his research that people who felt grateful would delay an immediate cash reward in favor of a bigger one later on. What's more, the degree of patience exhibited was directly related to the amount of gratitude any individual felt.

He says, "Gratitude and compassion have been tied to better academic performance, a greater willingness to exercise and eat healthily, and lower levels of consumerism, impulsivity, and tobacco and alcohol use. (DeSteno 2017)

A stronger, bionic you awaits.

When I was a little girl, young enough to wear a nightgown and back when my favorite thing in the world was birch beer, there was a TV series called *The Six Million Dollar Man* or, as we called it in our house, *The Bionic Man*. The series intro shows an astronaut crashing to Earth. The government implants robot parts to save his life and created a new man/half robot; thus, The Six Million Dollar Man.

In the opening sequence, a narrator (series producer Harve Bennett) identifies the protagonist, "Steve Austin, astronaut. A man barely alive." Richard Anderson, in character as Oscar Goldman, then intones off-camera, "Gentlemen, we can rebuild him. We have the technology. We have the capability to make the world's first bionic man. Steve Austin will be that man. Better than he was before. Better...stronger...faster" (Boyle 1978).

If I could implant you with gratitude and have it course through your veins, you too would be superhuman.

Better...stronger...faster.

And you do have the power to be better...stronger...faster simply by making the choice to practice gratitude.

In his book *Man's Search for Meaning*, Viktor Frankl writes: "Man is ultimately self-determining. What he becomes—within the limits of endowment and environment—he has made out of himself" (Frankl 1962).

The freedom to find our meaning is perhaps one of the most beautiful things about the human experience. Self-reflection and gratitude can help on this quest; gratitude is the mirror we hold up to our soul.

When you look in the mirror, who do you see? What part of your journey are you most grateful for?

THE EYE OF THE STORM

The view from the sixth floor of the hotel faced the Atlantic Ocean. Waves crashed onto the shore in a big white capped finish. The wind whipped and howled. We could feel the angry energy against the glass.

As an impending CAT 4 hurricane approached the West Coast of Florida, we had fled to the East Coast to wait out the storm. With the weather channel blasting on TV, we watched the big swirling eye of Hurricane Ian beat down on the coastline, our home and neighborhood. There was nothing we could do but pray.

The damage was devastating to areas south of our home. Bridges destroyed, entire neighborhoods with roofs ripped off, and houses flooded or gone forever. A few days later, we drove home and were rerouted several times from flooding. I gasped as we saw the rising waters, rivers spilled into communities, and caravans of the National Guard.

We were lucky the hurricane did not damage our house, but all around us, so much loss and pain. We heard of many families being displaced from their homes. A list of items needed went out and we decided to spend a weekend shopping for toothbrushes, clothing, and other basic needs and brought them to the distribution center for shelters. A group of my colleagues Venmoed me donations, and with what we also contributed, Ian, Liam, and I filled two truck beds.

We unloaded the items at the collection center. There were lines of cars with people who wanted to help. In the aftermath of natural disaster, it is beautiful to see how we as humans band together. After the hurricane, whenever we heard of others in need, we tried to Venmo or donate whatever we could.

Even the CEO of our company had major damage to his home. His entire first floor was flooded with the storm surge, and for days he wondered if his home might be a total loss; thankfully, it was not. But as he and his wife struggled to get it habitable, he said to me, "We will be okay. We have insurance. We have means. Yes, we have lost personal items we will never recover, but we will be able to fix things. I worry about those who have far less. They are the ones who need help."

During and after the storm, his constant priority was the needs of others.

One of our advisors in Tampa immediately started collecting donations for the shelters. Many others posted websites for hurricane relief to drum up awareness and help our communities. There was an outpouring of love and support. Over and over I heard, "How can we help?"

It is easy to wake up, have a cup of coffee, and go about your day and take it for granted. But when you realize so many around you woke up that same day without a place to live, it is extremely humbling.

My gratitudes shifted. I began to re-appreciate my home, my morning coffee, and the fact that I now had the ability to help others. There were times in my life that losing a fridge full of groceries to a power outage would have been a major financial burden. I was so grateful that not only could I restock the items in my fridge, but that I had the means to help others.

In times of great loss or disaster, gratitude becomes a life raft. It is plunked down in front of you and says, "Get in." Sometimes the crisis is public and sometimes it's private.

My friend and colleague Wendy is a cancer survivor. She told me, "Cancer doesn't come with benefits, except one: gratitude. Finding appreciation during this dark time helped heal me just as much as any of the medical treatments I endured." On her first day back to the office after her treatment, she was greeted with a massive flower arrangement.

Wendy recounts, "I literally had no place to put it. And then it hit me—I needed to pay it forward. I drove to the mammogram medical center, the place—the people—who had detected my cancer six weeks earlier. I felt strong and committed as I walked toward the receptionist carrying this absurdly enormous display of flowers. I told the entire medical team that they can never underestimate what they do. I expressed my sincere gratitude that they were well-trained and prepared to see this disease present itself early enough where I would live a long life with the privilege of continuing to be a wife, mother, daughter, sister, and friend." She added, "They helped me survive. I had to thank them."

Another good friend, Paige, battled cancer years ago and clung to gratitude as a life raft in a swirling ocean. After getting through the economic downturn of 2008, when she "lost everything," she had come out on the other side with her family and rebuilt their lives. They thrived.

She said, "And then one day I felt a lump in my neck. Fast forward, the oncologist said, 'We need to put you in a scanner.

Here's the address. It's in the basement of UK Hospital, University of Kentucky.' There are only two things in that basement: the morgue and the radiology department."

She was scared but used gratitude to cling to. Paige said, "I laid in the scanner and when you have head or neck cancer, it has to be so close it is almost touching your face. You have to lay there for an hour and a half while it scans you to decide if the cancer has traveled. In the scanner, instead of being afraid, I was grateful because of how far we had come. I was grateful we had health care. Grateful I needed to be there for my little boy. I chose gratitude because the other was not a choice for me. Because the alternative was to be in the morgue next door. But I chose life."

Paige beat cancer. She is one of the most kind and giving people I know. She still chooses gratitude in all things and it is very much a part of her daily habits.

I have learned that our scars remind us of what we have been through. They are not ugly or disfiguring, but in fact can be called "gratitude scars"; reminders that we have been fixed like the bionic man, that we have fought illness or death and persevered; we are still here to live another day.

Like Arya from *Game of Thrones* is told by her master swordfighter and instructor, Syrio Forel, "There is only one god, and His name is Death. And there is only one thing we say to Death: '*not today.*'"

Scars can be physical, but they can also be hidden. The scars of mental health trauma are real. I know many people, friends, and family members who struggle with mental illness. Although gratitude can't fix everything, it is used widely by clinical therapists and in residential treatment programs in conjunction with other treatment therapies. It can be a life raft for your struggles, no matter how troublesome.

Has gratitude ever been your life raft? Was there a moment in your life that gratitude magically appeared, and you said to yourself, "Get in"?

If so, how did that moment shape your life? What did gratitude do for you?

Gratitude Intervention

A gratitude intervention is like a shot in the arm of Vitamin G: it can change the way you think by regularly engaging in activities designed to "turn on" your gratitude switch. Intense gratitude activities for thirty days are considered a gratitude intervention.

GRATITUDE INTERVENTION
Jump-start your commitment or reengage with a month of gratitude.

- "Be Grateful" stickies on mirrors/surfaces.

- Morning and evening gratitude thoughts to self.

- Gratitude notepad/journal.

- Write thirty notes of gratitude to others in one month.

- Aim to use the words "I appreciate you" in every conversation.

- Tell strangers you meet (barista, waiter, mailman, delivery) you appreciate them.

- Perform random acts of kindness to spread gratitude.

- Tell the three most important people in your life you are thankful for them and why in a letter, text, or in person.

- Take a "Gratitude Challenge" by posting once a day for thirty days one thing (or person) you are grateful for and why on social media or in a group text.

In addition to the above, make gratitude a solution for stress. In the next thirty days, when you find yourself angry or stressed, flip on your gratitude switch.

Peter Parnegg is a coach and longtime real estate industry veteran. He says, "When you're feeling high stress, immediately turn your focus to something you're grateful for. It is this instantaneous ability to regain perspective. Gratitude is a hidden gem. It's a stress buster."

Trish Yan shared with me her story of daily gratitude: "I was going back to the Philippines in 1997, with no visa, no paperwork, and had no job. I was living in my aunt's house. I've had no furniture, no food, no money. And I gave myself the challenge of having to write ten things a day that I was grateful for. And some days it was very simple: thank god, I'm alive. I'm healthy. I'm breathing. I had one meal today."

Trish is now a successful coach and author. She is very blessed. A practice of gratitude was life-changing. She affirms, "I built that gratitude muscle over time. When I was down, or I was depressed, or I was stressed, or I was angry, I'd always turn to gratitude to instantly shift my energy or my mindset."

The purpose of a gratitude intervention is to jump-start your Habit of Grateful. Make the next thirty days count and jump in!

Easy Prompts for Gratitude Intervention

Use these prompts to help you find things to be grateful for if you get stuck.

- I'm grateful for three things I hear:

- I'm grateful for three things I see:

- I'm grateful for three things I smell

- I'm grateful for three things I touch/feel:

- I'm grateful for these three things I taste:

- I'm grateful for these three friends:

- I'm grateful for these three family members:

- I'm grateful for these three things in my home:

TIP

Calendar thirty days for a gratitude intervention. Choose what activities you will commit to. Find a buddy to enlist. Use this intervention to kick-start a Habit of Grateful. Take note how gratitude makes you feel. What have you learned?

TODAY

You are a gift to the world
and only you can share that gift.

TODAY is your chance. To give.

Be grateful that TODAY is an opportunity.
That you have unlimited potential.

The world is waiting for you.

TODAY you can change the lives of all those
you meet,
just by being YOU
(and that is a beautiful thing).

This is your life.

Be Grateful.
Be Kind.
Love.
Give.

TODAY.

The Afterglow

"Everything you can imagine is real."

—PABLO PICASSO

On the West Coast of Florida, *sunset is a thing.*

People will ask you if you want to "go watch sunset." It's a revered pastime, like going to a baseball game or movie. If you trek out to the beach about an hour before the big show, you will see all sorts of people sitting on blankets or chairs or just standing around. Some bring elaborate setups with tables, charcuterie boards, and wine glasses. Some just sip beer from a can.

Everyone waits for the sunset to start like a crowd ready for the opening act. There is a silent anticipation. A vibe.

Just past the clear blue gulf, the line between water and sky hushes the day away. The sun turns into a majestic red ball that sinks downward. It glows neon. Hot pink, sherbet orange. Everything is illuminated by streaks of color, and the water turns to silver tinged with fire. The sky lights up with infinite shades of red.

They say just before the sun sinks down entirely and disappears, there is a green flash of light; almost impossible to see. *Watch for it.*

As my feet touch the powdery sand, I am transfixed by the light show unfolding before me. My heart is so full in this moment. To witness such beauty is humbling and transformative all at once. If there is real magic, certainly this is what it looks like.

I am so grateful.

My kids have grown up in the flash of a thousand sunsets. Three are now adults. They are finding their way. I could not be prouder.

I think back to many years ago, to that cold winter we could not afford things like heat and food. I think back to the younger me, the one with the sad eyes; when I would stand in a crowd of people at a business function and not feel worthy. Like I did not belong.

It took me so many years to learn not only was I worthy of standing in that room, but I belonged in that room. Not because of my bank account, or the type of car I drove, but because I still have so much to give. There will always be room in this world for the givers.

Recently I was working on a visualization technique with my coach. You see, I still have work to do on myself. She guided me to close my eyes and to imagine myself back in time, at my old house, to the "old me."

"See yourself walking up to your old house. Go back in time to that front door."

"Wait, the old me?" I shuddered.

"Yes, the old you. Knock on the door. Does she answer?"

"Well, it takes some time because she thinks it's probably a bill collector. Not someone cool standing on her front porch."

My coach sighs. "Knock again. Does she answer?"

"Yes, she answers. She is young. And pretty, but she doesn't think it. She looks so...sad."

"And what does she think of future you?"

I pause.

"She is like...damn! Wow!"

"What do you need to say to the old you?" My coach asks. "Can you talk to her?"

This is tough.

I say, "I just want you to know you are stronger than you think. Find that fire in your belly. Believe in yourself. If I could just hand you my courage, I would, but I can't. You need to start believing in yourself. Accept that you are strong, you are smart, you are kind, and you are beautiful—inside and out. Not because anyone tells you this, but because *you* believe in yourself."

In that moment, I remember Mary's smile. She would be proud.

"And I want you to know someday your heart will be so full of gratitude that it will float over the sky like a big, fiery ball of energy. You will radiate pure love and color will fill the sky. The love of others, of those past and those present, will beam through you. *You* will do *great* things because you believe in yourself."

"Excellent," my coach says. "Now, I want you to say goodbye to that sad person. The old you. It's time to say goodbye to her. It's time to move on."

I feel the emotions well up inside my throat. In my mind I am standing inside my old house: the smell of pancakes and fresh-cut grass. The windows are open and a light spring breeze whispers through the curtains. The sweet voices of young kids. Cartoons on TV.

I stare at the old me. It occurs to me that I don't really know her that well anymore.

Sunset. The magic green flash. The sun leaves us to make room for what's coming next. And it's okay, because we all know that tomorrow, the sun will rise again.

"Goodbye," I say to the old me. "I won't be coming back here."

Before I turn to leave, I hug her tight.

I whisper, "*Thank you.*"

When the sun finally disappears, it leaves an afterglow. Everyone claps.

The sky is different. The hues of red soften. This is when the crowds leave the beach and we pack up our chairs, our cooler, and head home. Every time I see a sunset, I think:

Have I given to others today?

How many more sunsets will I have?

I always look for the gratitudes and for all the blessings from that day. I am lucky to have so many; it's like the sunset left a treasure chest in the sand just for me.

For us.

Acknowledgments

Thank you to New Degree Press and Eric Koester. Erinn Kemper, you are an incredible editor and saved me. Mike Butler, thanks for your editing and encouragement. To Trish Yan for nudging me into this project: super grateful!

Some *big* thanks to: my special family at PSIR, especially Budge Huskey; my peeps at WPSIR and everyone at SIR, and my fellow BIG SIR Thinkers: you guys all rock.

To *Ninja Selling*, especially Larry Kendall and Peter Parnegg, thank you for changing lives (and mine).

To Bob Burg and Kathy Tagenel, you are truly the biggest givers in the world.

To my cheering section: Melanie Frank, Maria Vitale, Lisa Piccardo, Colleen Barry, Jennifer Roller, Kim Knox, Kristen Conroy, Jim Miller, and Wes Madden. And, of course, Mary Dineen. I would not be here without your support.

To Chris Klug, Melissa Wandall, Dawn Rousseau, and everyone else who shared their stories, thank you from the bottom of my heart.

Thank you to my parents, Tom and Karen, and my bonus parents, Gene and Suzanne.

To my children, Triston, Jacob, Amelia, and Liam, as well as my new daughter-in-law, Rach.

And to the love of my life, Ian.

And butter.

Appendix

INTRODUCTION

Emmons, Robert. 2013. *Gratitude Works!: A 21-Day Program for Creating Emotional Prosperity.* San Francisco: Jossey-Bass.

WHAT IS GRATITUDE

Allen, Summer. 2018. "The Science of Gratitude." A white paper prepared for the John Templeton Foundation by the Greater Good Science Center at UC Berkeley, Online, May 2018 https://ggsc.berkeley.edu/images/uploads/GGSC-JTF_White_ Paper-Gratitude-FINAL.pdf.

Chowdhury, Madhuleena. 2019. "The Neuroscience of Gratitude and Effects on the Brain." *Grief & Bereavement* (blog), *PositivePsychology.com.* April 9, 2019. https:// positivepsychology.com/neuroscience-of-gratitude/.

Emmons, Robert. 2013. *Gratitude Works!: A 21-Day Program for Creating Emotional Prosperity.* San Francisco: Jossey-Bass.

Emmons, Robert, and McCullough, Michael. 2004. *The Psychology of Gratitude.* New York: Oxford University Press. Google Play Books.

Lambert, Nathaniel. 2019. "A Prototype Analysis of Gratitude: Varieties of Gratitude Experiences." *Personality and Social Psychology Bulletin* 35, no. 9 (September): 1193–1207. https://doi.org/10.1177/0146167209338071.

ANCIENT HISTORY I
Gilbert, Elizabeth. 2019 "Elizabeth_gilbert_writer." Instagram. Accessed September 1st, 2022. https://www.instagram.com/p/B3PlmZMBfMo/

WHAT DOES GRATITUDE MEAN TO YOU?
Akers, Alicia. 2022. "Is Gen Z More Depressed?" *Medical News Today* (blog). March 24, 2022. https://www.medicalnewstoday.com/articles/why-is-gen-z-depressed.

ANCIENT HISTORY II
Marston, Ralph. 2021. "The Daily Motivator." *Thankful For You*, November 25, 2021. https://greatday.com/motivate/211125.html.

POSITIVE MINDSET
Achor, Shawn. 2018. *The Happiness Advantage*. New York: Currency.

Emmons, Robert. 2003. "Counting Blessings Versus Burdens: An Experimental Investigation of Gratitude and Subjective Well-Being in Daily Life." *Journal of Personality and Social Psychology* 84, no. 2 (September): 377–389.

Fredrickson, Barbara. 2013. "Chapter One—Positive Emotions Broaden and Build." *Advances in Experimental Social Psychology* 47, no. 1 (April): 1–53. https://doi.org/10.1016/B978-0-12-407236-7.00001-2.

Hill, Patrick. 2013. "Examining the Pathways between Gratitude and Self-Rated Physical Health across Adulthood." *Personality and Individual Differences* 54, no. 1 (January): 92–96. https://doi.org/10.1016/j.paid.2012.08.011.

Krause, Neal. 2015. "Humility, Compassion, and Gratitude to God: Assessing the Relationships Among Key Religious Virtues." *Psychology of Religion and Spirituality* 7, no. 3 (August): 192–204. https://doi.org/10.1037/rel0000028.

Marquand, Richard, director. *Star Wars. Episode VI, Return of the Jedi.* Twentieth Century Fox Home Entertainment, 2013. 136 min.

McCraty, Rollin. 1995. "The Effects of Emotions on Short-Term Power Spectrum Analysis of Heart Rate Variability." *The American Journal of Cardiology* 76, no. 14 (November): 1089–1093. https://doi.org/10.1016/S0002-9149(99)80309-9.

Mccullough, Michael, Robert Emmons, and Jo-Ann Tsang. 2002. "The Grateful Disposition: A Conceptual and Empirical Topography." *Journal of Personality and Social Psychology* 82, no. 1 (January): 112–127. https://psycnet.apa.org/doi/10.1037/0022-3514.82.1.112.

Tony, Team. 2022. "What is an Abundance Mindset?" *Mind & Meaning* (blog), *The Tony Robbins Blog.* https://www.tonyrobbins.com/mind-meaning/adopt-abundance-mindset/.

Witvliet, Charlotte vanOyen, Fallon J. Richie, Lindsey M. Root Luna, and Daryl R. Van Tongeren. 2018. "Gratitude Predicts Hope and Happiness: A Two-Study Assessment of Traits and States" *The Journal of Positive Psychology.* (January): 271–282. https://doi.org/10.1080/17439760.2018.1424924.

Zahn, Roland. 2008. "The Neural Basis of Human Social Values: Evidence from Functional MRI." *Cereb Cortex* 19, no. 2 (May): 276–283. https://doi.org/10.1093%2Fcercor%2Fbhn080.

Zahn, Roland, Griselda Garrido, Jorge Moll, and Jordan Grafman. 2014. "Individual Differences in Posterior Cortical Volume Correlate with Proneness to Pride and Gratitude." *Social Cognitive and Affective Neuroscience* 9, no. 11 (November): 1676–1683. https://doi.org/10.1093/scan/nst158.

Zahn, Roland, Jorge Moll, Vijeth Iyengar, Edward D. Huey, Michael Tierney, Frank Krueger, and Jordan Grafman. 2009. "Social Conceptual Impairments in Frontotemporal Lobar Degeneration with Right Anterior Temporal Hypometabolism." *Brain* 132, no. 3: 604–616.

DIG

Singh, Manoj. 2022. "The 2007–2008 Financial Crisis in Review." *Markets* (blog), *Investopedia.* September 18, 2022. https://www.investopedia.com/articles/economics/09/financial-crisis-review.asp

STRONGER

Cascio, Christopher. 2015. "Self-Affirmation Activates Brain Systems Associated with Self-Related Processing and Reward and is Reinforced by Future Orientation." *Social Cognitive and Affective Neuroscience* 11, no. 4 (November): 621–629. https://doi.org/10.1093/scan/nsv136.

Digital, Glitch. 2021. "Jim Carrey's Law of Attraction and Visualization Tips." *General* (blog), *Influencive*. June 23, 2021. https://www.influencive.com/jim-carreys-law-of-attraction-and-visualization-tips/.

Epic, Most. 2020. "Jim Carrey Talks about the Law of Attraction on Oprah Show (1997)." YouTube. July 17, 2020. 2:16. https://www.youtube.com/watch?v=414zgW-S_YE.

Kromer, Ed. 2020. "How to Cultivate Gratitude During Difficult Times—and Why It Can Make Us All Feel Better." *Faculty* (blog), *Foster Blog*. March 24, 2020. https://blog.foster.uw.edu/cultivate-gratitude-difficult-times/.

Maslow, Abraham. 1943. "A Theory of Human Motivation." *Psychological Review* 50, no. 4 (July): 370–396. https://doi.org/10.1037/h0054346.

Mjaaset, Nina. 2022. "A Deep Dive into the Science behind Self-Affirmations." *Beauty* (blog), *Vogue*. May 2, 2022. https://www.vogue.in/beauty/content/a-deep-dive-into-the-science-behind-self-affirmations.

MORNING ROUTINE

Emmons, Robert. 2003. "Counting Blessings Versus Burdens: An Experimental Investigation of Gratitude and Subjective

Well-Being in Daily Life." *Journal of Personality and Social Psychology* 84, no. 2 (September): 377–389.

Happy & Well. 2012. "Martin Seligman 'Flourishing—A New Understanding of Well-Being' at Happiness and Its Causes 2012." YouTube. August 26, 2012. 30:07. https://www.youtube.com/watch?v=eoLbwEVnfJA.

Pangambam, S. 2016. "Louie Schwartzberg on Gratitude at TEDxSF (Full Transcript)." *Life & Relationships* (blog), *The Singju Post*. April 12, 2016. https://singjupost.com/louie-schwartzberg-on-gratitude-at-tedxsf-full-transcript/.

Pursuit-of-Happiness.org. 2022. "Martin Seligman." Pursuit of Happiness. August, 2022. https://www.pursuit-of-happiness.org/history-of-happiness/martin-seligman-psychology/.

TED. 2013. "Want to Be Happy? Be Grateful—David Steindl-Rast." June 2013 in Edinburgh, Scotland. Video, 14:30. https://ed.ted.com/lessons/3foo5sIG.

Xander, Michael, and Spall, Benjamin. 2014. "James Clear." My Morning Routine. August, 2022. https://mymorningroutine.com/james-clear/.

COLD HEART

Crowe, Cameron, director. 1996. *Jerry Maguire*. United States: TriStar Pictures.

Gilbert, Elizabeth. 2007. *Eat, Pray, Love*. New York: Riverhead Books.

Maslow, A.H. 1943. A Theory of Human Motivation. *Psychological Review* 50, no. 4: 370–96.

McLeod, Saul. 2007. "Maslow's Hierarchy of Needs." *SimplyPsychology* (blog). April 4, 2022. https://www. simplypsychology.org/maslow.html.

Somewhere Else for Something Else. 2011. "Jerry Maguire— 'Shoplift the Pootie.'" YouTube. October 8, 2011. 1:22. https:// www.youtube.com/watch?v=SsMV3uNaTpU.

HABIT #2

Chowdhury, Madhuleena. Publication Year. "The Neuroscience of Gratitude and Effects on the Brain." *Grief & Bereavement* (blog), *PositivePsychology.com*. April 9, 2019. https:// positivepsychology.com/neuroscience-of-gratitude

Fletcher, Emily. 2017. "The Neuroscience of Gratitude." *HuffPost*. Dec 6, 2017. https://www.huffpost.com/entry/the-neuroscience-of-gratitude_b_8631392

Hanh, Thich. 2017. *The Art of Living*. London: Random House UK.

Patterson, Kerry, Joseph Grenny, Ron McMillan, and Al Switzler. *Crucial Conversations: Tools for Talking When Stakes Are High*. New York: McGraw Hill, 2021.

Schulz, Jodi. 2018. "Gratitude Part 1: What Is It and How Do I Include It in My Life." *Michigan State University Extension* (blog). May 1, 2018. https://www.canr.msu.edu/news/gratitude_ part_1_what_is_it_and_how_do_i_include_it_in_my_life.

LEADING WITH GRATITUDE

Carnegie, Dale. 1998. *How to Win Friends & Influence People.* New York: Gallery Books.

Kendall, Larry. 2017. *Ninja Selling.* Austin: Greenleaf Book Group Press.

Lencioni, Patrick. 2016. *The Ideal Team Player.* Hoboken: Jossey-Bass. Kindle.

HABIT #3

Editors at Chopra.com. 2012. "Cultivate the Healing Power of Gratitude." *Personal Growth* (blog), *Chopra.* November 3, 2012. https://chopra.com/articles/cultivate-the-healing-power-of-gratitude.

Simon-Thomas, Emiliana. 2012. "A 'Thnx' a Day Keeps the Doctor Away." *Mind & Body* (blog), *Greater Good Magazine.* December 19, 2012. https://greatergood.berkeley.edu/article/item/a_thnx_a_day_keeps_the_doctor_away.

Toepfer, Steven, Kelly Cichy, and Patti Peters 2012. *Letters of Gratitude: Further Evidence for Author Benefits.* Journal of Happiness Studies 13: 187–201. 10.1007/s10902-011-9257-7.

Wood, Alex. 2009. "Gratitude Influences Sleep Through the Mechanism of Pre-Sleep Cognitions." *Journal of Psychosomatic Research* 66, no. 1 (January): 43–48.

Frankl, Viktor E. 1962. *Man's Search for Meaning : an Introduction to Logotherapy.* Boston: Beacon Press.

THE ROAD TO GRATITUDE: A MAP

Ackerman, Courtney. 2018. "What Is Positive Psychology and Why Is It Important?" *Theory & Books* (blog), *PositivePsychology.com*. April 20, 2018. https://positivepsychology.com/what-is-positive-psychology-definition

Emmons, Robert A. 2007. *Thanks!: How the New Science of Gratitude Can Make You Happier*. New York: Houghton Mifflin Company.

Farr, Adrienne. 2022. "Five Ways to Boost Your Gratitude." *Your Healthiest Self* (blog), *Oprah Daily*. October 14, 2022. https://www.oprahdaily.com/life/health/a41611771/intentions-boost-your-gratitude/.

Hanson, Rick. 2007. "Gratitude." RickHanson.net. Accessed October 30, 2022. https://www.rickhanson.net/gratitude-2/.

Kozlowska, Kasia. Peter Walker. Loyola McLean. Pascal Carrive. 2015. "Fear and the Defense Cascade: Clinical Implications and Management." *Harv Rev Psychiatry* 23, no. 4 (Jul–Aug): 263–87. doi: 10.1097/HRP.0000000000000065.

Peterson, Christopher. 2008. "What Is Positive Psychology and What Is It Not?" *Positive Psychology* (blog), *Psychology Today*. May 16, 2008. https://www.psychologytoday.com/us/blog/the-good-life/200805/what-is-positive-psychology-and-what-is-it-not.

Schmitz, Taylor. 2009. "Opposing Influences of Affective State Valence on Visual Cortical Encoding." *Journal of Neuroscience* 29, no. 22 (June): 7199–7207. https://doi.org/10.1523/JNEUROSCI.5387-08.2009.

Seligman, Martin. 2005. "Positive Psychology Progress: Empirical Validation of Interventions." *American Psychologist* 60, no. 5 (Jul-Aug): 410–421. https://doi.org/10.1037/0003-066x.60.5.410.

Smith, Ian, director. 2018. Larry King Now "Martin Seligman on Happiness, PTSD, and a Cure for Depression." Ora TV. 27 min. https://youtu.be/43zvL2b10D4.

Woods, Rob. 2021. "Rose-Colored Glasses Show Us the World in a Better Light." *Resources* (blog), *All About Vision*. February 3, 2021. https://www.allaboutvision.com/resources/human-interest/rose-colored-glasses-history-function.

WALK YOUR WAY TO GRATEFUL

Rickman, Cheryl. 2013. "Walking into Well-Being: The Power of the Gratitude Walk." *Healthy Living* (blog), *HuffPost*. November 10, 2013. https://www.huffingtonpost.co.uk/cheryl-rickman/walking-and-wellbeing_b_3902687.html.

Schwartzberg, Louie. 2022. "Biography." MovingArt.com. October 1, 2022. https://movingart.com/louie-schwartzberg-filmmaker

Strayed, Cheryl. 2012. *Wild*. New York: Alfred A. Knopf. Kindle.

MARY

Burg, Bob. 2015. *The Go-Giver, Expanded Edition: A Little Story About a Powerful Business Idea*. New York: Penguin.

Emmons, Robert. 2010. "Why Gratitude Is Good." *Mind & Body* (blog), *Greater Good Magazine*. November 16 2010. https://greatergood.berkeley.edu/article/item/why_gratitude_is_good.

HABIT #4

Brown, Brené. 2019. "Gwyneth x Brené Brown: On the Roots of Shame, Courage, and Vulnerability." Gwyneth Paltrow. *The Goop Podcast*. April 18, 2019. 1:04. https://goop.com/the-goop-podcast/gwyneth-x-brene-brown-on-the-roots-of-shame-courage-and-vulnerability/.

Editors at Chopra.com. 2012. "Cultivate the Healing Power of Gratitude." *Personal Growth* (blog), *Chopra*. November 3, 2012. https://chopra.com/articles/cultivate-the-healing-power-of-gratitude.

Emmons, Robert. 2016. *The Little Book of Gratitude*. Great Britain: Gaia.

Mills, Paul J., Laura Redwine, Kathleen Wilson, Meredith A. Pung, Kelly Chinh, Barry H. Greenberg, Ottar Lunde, Alan Maisel, Ajit Raisinghani, Alex Wood, and Deepak Chopra. 2015. "The Role of Gratitude in Spiritual Well-Being in Asymptomatic Heart Failure Patients." *Spirituality in Clinical Practice* 2, no. 1 (2015): 5–17. doi:10.1037/scp0000050.

Ng, Mei-Yee, and Wing-Sze Wong. 2013. "The Differential Effects of Gratitude and Sleep on Psychological Distress in Patients with Chronic Pain." *Journal of Health Psychology* 18, no. 2 (2013): 263–71. doi:10.1177/1359105312439733.

The Eye of the Storm

Boyle, Cliff, director. 1978. *The Six Million Dollar Man*. Universal Playback. Opening. https://www.youtube.com/watch?v=oCPJ-AbCsT8

DeSteno, David. 2017. "The Only Way to Keep Your Resolutions/ Gray Matter." *New York Times*. Accessed October 10, 2022. https://www.nytimes.com/2017/12/29/opinion/sunday/the-only-way-to-keep-your-resolutions.html

Karen, Julie. 2022. "Basal Cell Carcinoma Overview." Skin Cancer Foundation. August 2022. https://www.skincancer.org/skin-cancer-information/basal-cell-carcinoma

Lindley, Jennifer. 2018. "How to Practice Gratitude for a Healthier, Happier Life." *Life* (blog), *Prevention*. November 20, 2018. https://www.prevention.com/life/a25241089/benefits-of-gratitude

Williamson, M. 1996. *A Return to Love*. United Kingdom: HarperCollins.